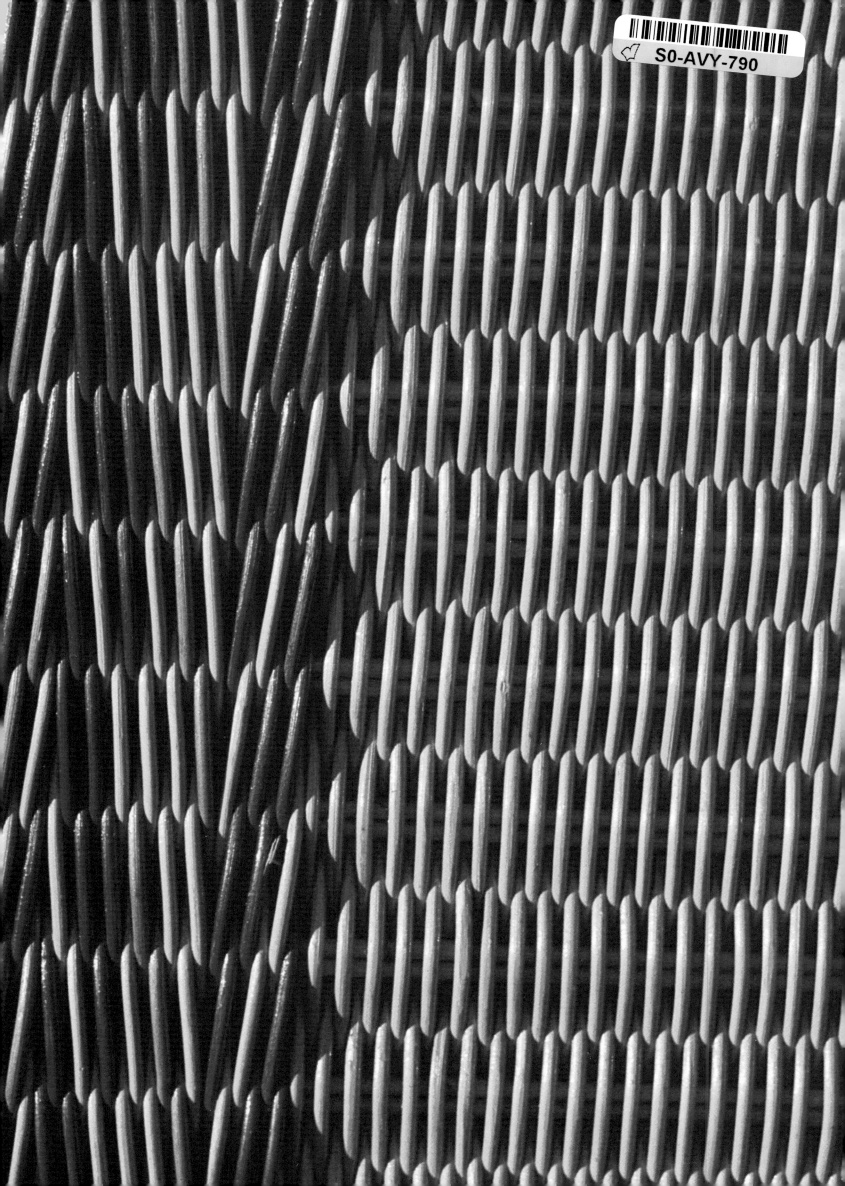

The
Great
Balloon
Festival

This Copy of

The Great
Balloon Festival

is Presented to

_____

_____

_____

_____

_____

_____

From

_____

Walla Walla Balloon Stampede
Ed Dosien

The Great Balloon Festival

A Season of Hot Air Balloon Meets Across North America

Principal Photography by Ed Dosien
Text by Joe Nigg
Design by Bob Brown
Foreword by Dave Liniger

FREE
FLIGHT
PRESS

Free Flight Press, Inc.
Englewood, Colorado

Copyright ©1989, Free Flight Press, Inc.
All rights reserved
First printing
Printed in the United States of America

Library of Congress Catalog Card Number: 88-083831

Free Flight Press, Inc.
P.O. Box 3907
Englewood, Colorado 80155-3907

Free Flight Press, Inc.,
is a trade name of RE/MAX International, Inc.,
a network of independently owned and operated
real estate offices.

Contents

Foreword *by Dave Liniger*
Preface

Pre-Flight

The Great Balloon Festival

Post-Flight

For her enthusiasm, her entrepreneurial vision,
and her indomitable spirit in the face of overwhelming odds,
this book is affectionately dedicated to
Gail Liniger,
President of RE/MAX International

At the age of 27, Gail Liniger co-founded the RE/MAX International real estate franchise network. Throughout the early days of that struggling young entrepreneurial company, her intelligence, enthusiasm, tenacity, and leadership guided the development of the organization.

The promise of those vital years, though, dimmed in 1983. On October 22nd of that year, Gail was critically injured when the small plane in which she was riding on RE/MAX business crashed in a Canadian pine forest.

Over the next many months, Gail's own sheer courage and indomitable will struggled against seemingly impossible odds, eventually resulting in her recovery. Her return to daily work as a part of her own rehabilitation made her a figure of inspiration throughout the RE/MAX International system.

Aided by her untiring efforts, the RE/MAX organization has continued to expand until it is now one of the largest, most successful real estate networks in the world.

Gail's remarkable triumph over adversity is the perfect symbol of the RE/MAX "Above the Crowd!®" spirit.

Foreword

Hot air balloons have been special to RE/MAX International ever since we became associated with them back in 1978.

At that time, we were in the first phase of franchising our network of real estate offices across North America, and we had only several hundred people in the system. Corporate balloons were becoming popular then, and our Regional Directors in New Mexico decided to spread the RE/MAX name in their area by creating a RE/MAX balloon and flying it at the famous Albuquerque Fiesta. They designed a red, white, and blue balloon with the RE/MAX logotype on it, and an associate of theirs devised the "Above the Crowd!®" slogan for crew jackets. Their new advertising tool was delivered just in time for the Fiesta, the balloon flew, and the RE/MAX name started to be known around Albuquerque. After learning of the New Mexico balloon promotion, we at International Headquarters began exploring the marketing uses of balloons throughout the system.

In the Denver area, our organization was number one in listings and sales even then, but according to a public poll regarding real estate companies, we were number eight in recognition. We decided it was time to debut the RE/MAX Balloon in our area, so we purchased a balloon and featured it in a television commercial. After the commercial was aired in the Denver area over a period of four months, our recognition rating rocketed straight up to number one.

Due to the dramatic marketing impact of our commercial, our advertising agency highly recommended we adopt the red, white, and blue balloon image as a corporate logo. We immediately recognized that a hot air balloon flying free "Above the Crowd!" represented everything our organization had set out to be. We could see that the logo graphically embodied the independence, freedom, and professionalism we had wished to foster with our RE/MAX high-commission concept from the time we founded the organization in 1973. We adopted the new logo on all corporate materials.

Since that time, the RE/MAX Hot Air Balloon Fleet has expanded right along with our organization. We are now an international leader in the real estate industry – due in large part to the advertising success of the RE/MAX Balloon image – and we now have scores of RE/MAX Hot Air Balloons in the system, the largest corporate balloon fleet anywhere. Now, millions of people across North America cannot possibly see a red, white, and blue RE/MAX Hot Air Balloon without thinking of the RE/MAX organization itself.

While we were building our balloon fleet for business purposes, something happened that we did not necessarily anticipate: Like thousands of people before us, we fell under the spell of balloons, those wonderful gentle giants. As balloonists are fond of saying, "Everybody loves a balloon." We certainly did. We also liked balloonists, who are similar to other successful people in their habitual enthusiasm and optimism. We liked the professionalism of the corporate pilots and the family cooperation of crews. We liked being part of the corporate balloon community. And finally, we liked the color and the communal spirit of festivals.

In all, we liked ballooning so much we decided to produce an extensive photograph book on the subject. First of all, it is difficult to imagine anything more photogenic than a multi-colored balloon, and secondly, we could find no other balloon book on the scale we wanted to publish. To us, ballooning deserved an elaborate photographic treatment.

This book embraces an entire ballooning season. The highlight of the book, of course, is photographs of balloons themselves – being inflated, launching, flying, landing. As balloonists stress, though, much of the appeal of the sport for them is being with other balloonists and providing excitement and enjoyment for the spectators, so people play a big part in the photographs that follow. Then there are concessions, midways, activities – everything that makes balloon festivals the wonderful events they are.

Our production crew traveled across the United States and Canada throughout the hot air balloon season, attending nearly twenty festivals in all, taking nearly 50,000 photographs and reams of notes. Along the way – at nearly every one of the meets – RE/MAX pilots, crews, or RE/MAX Associates were there to help out. We extend our warmest appreciation to all those RE/MAX people who contributed behind the scenes to make this book the ultimate hot air balloon festival in pictures and words.

I can think of no better way to celebrate ten years of the RE/MAX Hot Air Balloon and to honor the magnificent sport of ballooning itself than by offering this book to balloon-lovers everywhere.

Dave Liniger
Chief Executive Officer
RE/MAX International, Inc.

Preface

When the Norse god Odin would arrive on foot at an ocean shore, he would pull a package out of his pouch, unfold the material to its full, longship form, board the vessel, and sail away. No less magical than Odin's ship is a hot air balloon envelope. In the balloonist's envelope bag is stuffed a piece of cloth which, when it is filled with heat, is as tall as a seven-story building and yet is lighter than air. It can be any color – or combination of colors – on earth. It can be the shape of a newspaper, a house, a flying saucer, a gas pump, an elephant. You can fly in it for fun. You can fly other people in it for money. You can fly it in international competition. You can fly it to advertise a commercial product. Whenever you fly it, and for whatever reason, nearly anyone who sees it will watch it with delight – and even wonder. After you've landed, you roll it up and stuff it back in its bag, much the way Odin did with his ship when he reached the far shore.

One of the few things more enchanting to watch than one hot air balloon is two hot air balloons, and so on, right up to the several hundred balloons which lift off in a mass ascension at the annual Albuquerque Hot Air Balloon Fiesta. To see other people rise into the air under these fabric bubbles, hundreds of thousands of people each year do what they would not think of doing for most things in life: rise around four o'clock on a Saturday morning and drive miles through the dark, drawing near their destination only to be stuck in a traffic jam with other people doing the same thing for the same reason.

The publishers of *The Great Balloon Festival* recognized that hot air balloon festivals are a unique social phenomenon and they wanted to create a photograph book which would show what spectators see at these events. First, what those people see is one of the most colorful, most aesthetically pleasing sights anywhere: hot air balloons – in inflation, in launch, in flight. While balloons themselves are certainly a fitting subject for a collection of photographs, the publishers also wanted to include the other dimensions of a balloon meet: the pilots and crews, the spectators, the midway concessions, the festival activities, the barbecues. In all, what they wanted to produce was a complete hot air balloon festival between book covers.

To do that, they sent our production team – photographer Ed Dosien, art director Bob Brown, photographer's assistant John Liniger, and myself as writer – to hot air balloon meets across North America throughout the standard April-to-October ballooning season. Out of about 150 scheduled meets in the United States and Canada, nearly twenty were chosen to represent the great variety of size, type, and location of hot air balloon festivals.

By the time the balloon book team had attended the climactic Albuquerque Hot Air Balloon Fiesta in early October, principal photographer Ed Dosien – after scores of balloon flights and hundreds of hours among festival crowds – had produced a massive library of balloon photography, only a fraction of which could be used in a normal-sized book. It was the formidable yet enviable task of art director and designer Bob Brown to select from the thousands of photographs the several hundred which would be used in this book. It should be stressed that photographic integrity and fidelity to the subjects shot demanded that all the photographs are what the camera saw and recorded; they are not computerized composites of photographs, nor have their colors been radically adjusted during the separation process.

For the sake of unity and dramatic development, we have arranged the photographs taken over the entire season into a single festival, as though it were occurring simultaneously across the North American continent. The reader interested in identifying the photographer who took any given photograph or the meet at which any photograph was taken need only consult the credit lines beside the picture.

By its very nature, the book creates its own variation of a typical balloon festival day. A standard balloon meet day consists of pilot briefings at twelve-hour intervals – at, say, 5:30 a.m. and 5:30 p.m. – and flights scheduled an hour or so later, with festival activities running throughout the day between flights and into the night. Normally, pilots and crews rise around 4 a.m., eat a brunch after the first flight of the day, nap, return to the launch field in late afternoon, and eat a late dinner after the afternoon flight. A few hours' sleep, and back up in the middle of the night. It is a grueling schedule. For the flow of the book and the enjoyment of the reader, though, flights continue throughout the day.

This book could not have existed in its present form without the help of a great many people, especially balloon pilots and crews and festival administrators who created photographic opportunities for photographer Ed Dosien or contributed ballooning information and stories to the author. First, we would like to give special thanks to balloon pilot Russ McLain and other "Flying McLains" – John, Ruth, and Scott – for all the flights and crewing, for their wonderful stories about ballooning, and for warmly initiating us into their lighter-than-air world. I extend my appreciation to their long-time balloonist friend Chauncey Dunn for his balloon lore; and I would like to thank those four distinguished balloonists who so generously shared their experiences and time with me for the historical section of the text: Jean-Paul Frachon, Ed Yost, Don Piccard, and Sid Cutter.

The book production crew would like to thank the following people for their considerable contributions to this project: Balloonists Greg Ashton, Jean Beauregard, Mario Bilodeau, Ron Briley, Tom Bergeon, Roy Caton, Hakan Colting, Bruce Comstock, Dennis "Captain Phogg" Flodden, Michael Gernat, Allan Gnadt, Ron Groce, Gilbert Fontaine, Larry Fowell, Willard Hibbard, Will Jacoby, Earl Kapty, Lisa Kempner, Larry Knight, Ken Lovell, Steve Mroz, Jerry Nelson, Pat Roddy, Dave Ryan, Jim Ryan, Joel Sturdevant, Scott Spencer, Ed VandeHoef, Chris Van Dis, and Paul Woessner; Festival Administrators Catherine Barette, Sharon Benson, Barbara Brenner, William Cone, Sybil Goruk, Delbert Deschambault, Nanc Reznicek, and Debbie Spaes; and all the others who helped us along the way.

Most of the text in this book was derived from conversations and observation, precluding the need for a formal bibliography. I am particularly indebted, though, to Donald Dale Jackson's *The Aeronauts* and Dick Wirth's *Ballooning* for historical information used between interviews in the "From Annonay to Albuquerque" segment of this book. For those readers wanting additional information on ballooning, I recommend the following books as an entry to the subject: L.T.C. Rolt's *The Romance of Ballooning: The Story of the Aeronauts*, C. Burton Cosgrove's *Fantasy of Flight*, Erik Norgaard's *The Book of Ballooning*, and Dr. Will Hayes's *Balloon Digest*. Donald Dale Jackson's *The Aeronauts* contains a comprehensive bibliography of books about ballooning.

Joe Nigg

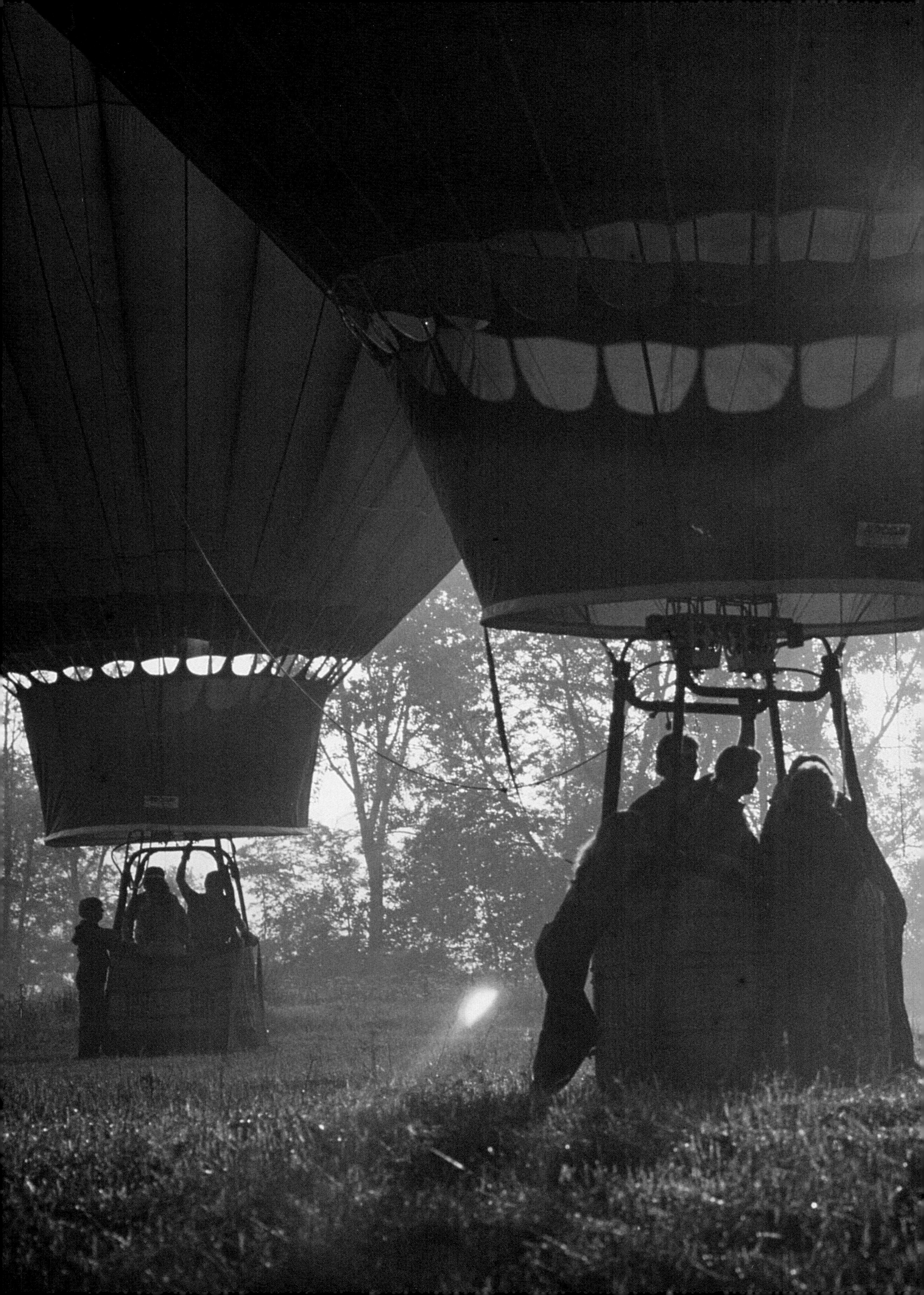

On the Air
Ed Dosien

Pre-Flight
A Short Oral History of Hot Air Ballooning

"Promptly prepare a provision of taffeta and ropes, and you will see one of the most incredible things in the world." This line in a letter from Joseph Montgolfier to his brother Etienne, in 1782, represents the birth of ballooning, the realization of mankind's centuries-old dream of flight. Four balloonists – a descendent of the Montgolfier brothers, the "Father of Modern Hot Air Ballooning," the first promoter of the sport, and the founder of the grandest gathering of balloons in the world – tell how the hot air balloon developed into the colorful marvel it is today.

9

From Annonay to Albuquerque
A Short Oral History of Hot Air Ballooning

Human beings flew in the imagination before they flew in air. In myths and folktales around the world, men and women escape the bonds of earth as easily as birds and drift as freely as the clouds. They ride giant eagles and winged horses. They rise in baskets pulled upward by gryphons. They wear wings of their own. They sit on magic carpets. Sometimes they fly just by stretching out their arms. In the mind, there is virtually no end to the ways we can rise into the sky.

Devising actual ways to join the birds took longer, and when we did, we first floated like clouds, lighter than air. Fixed-wing aircraft, imitating bird forms, did not fly until more than a hundred years after the first balloons rose in France near the end of the 18th century.

Hot air ballooning, begun more than two centuries ago, has actually been a sport for less than fifty years. Cumbersome hot air balloons were all but forgotten through the 19th century, while gas balloons were flown for recreation and entertainment and used in warfare and scientific research. Years of experimentation with envelope fabric, burners, and fuel systems led to the 1960 flight of the first modern hot air balloon. Now – even in the age of space exploration and footprints on the moon – hot air balloons draw millions of people each year to festivals in North America, Europe, Japan, and other places around the world. What those millions go to watch is what the imagination saw first: the spectacle of human beings rising into the air.

The reminiscences below informally trace the development of the hot air balloon, the *montgolfiere*. Balloonists Jean-Paul Frachon, Ed Yost, Don Piccard, and Sid Cutter have all been intimately connected with some chapter of the story of ballooning. Overall, their accounts follow the hot air balloon from its beginnings in Annonay, France, to the largest and most famous gathering of balloons anywhere, the Albuquerque International Hot Air Balloon Fiesta. Once the reader has made that same journey, he or she will be all the more prepared to attend the Great Balloon Festival in the photographs that follow.

The reader might be cautioned, however, by Don Piccard's observation that, "Talking with balloonists is just like flying a balloon: You don't know where you're going, and when you get there, you don't know where you've been."

Jean-Paul Frachon
The Origins of the Montgolfiere

1783 was a year of marvels. After centuries of unsuccessful schemes and attempts to carry human beings into the air, two different varieties of manned aircraft – the hot air balloon and the gas balloon – flew within ten days of each other.

Throughout the year, Joseph and Etienne Montgolfier sent up their hot air balloons on unmanned flights, a free flight with barnyard animals, and tethered manned flights. Because they thought that smoke rather than heat made the fabric globes rise, the fires in their balloons were stoked with wet straw, sheep's wool,

decomposing meat, anything which would create an abundance of smoke. At the same time, Jacques Alexander Cesar Charles was experimenting with gas balloons, which were given lift by the newly-discovered gas, hydrogen.

When King Louis XVI heard that the Montgolfier brothers were planning a manned flight of their balloon, he decreed that criminals should be the first to go up in the new invention, because they were expendable. A young nobleman, Pilatre de Rozier, objected, saying that the honor of being the first human to fly should belong to a gentleman. Near the end of November 1783, de Rozier and the Marquis d'Arlandes became the world's first aeronauts when they rose from the earth in the Montgolfiers' blue sphere decorated with the golden face of the sun god Apollo. D'Arlandes later wrote that as they drifted over Paris, he was astonished by the silence. The two men fed the fire at the base of the balloon with straw, setting the balloon fabric on fire, and extinguished the flames with a sponge and a bucket of water. Twenty-five minutes after launching, they landed gently, five miles away from where they had lifted off. A week and a half later, Professor Charles and Noel Robert launched their gas balloon from the Tuileries, touched down twenty-seven miles away, and after Robert climbed out, Charles ascended again, to such an altitude that he saw his second sunset that day.

The following account of these events is compiled from "family documents and stories" by Jean-Paul Frachon, a distant relative of Joseph and Etienne Montgolfier. Since the late 1960s, Frachon has worked for the company which owns the Vidalon paper mill, near Annonay, the same factory at which first Joseph, then Etienne, experimented with cloth, paper, and smoke, devising their first balloons. Frachon explained that the Vidalon paper mill was started around 1557 by the Chelles family. In 1693, Michel and Raymond Montgolfier, from the paper mill of Beaujeu, married two of the Chelles daughters, and later, Pierre Montgolfier, son of Raymond and father of Joseph and Etienne, ran the business. Today, the paper mill manufactures about 30,000 tons of high-quality drawing paper per year and also makes cardboard for advertising and publishing uses. The factory employs 500 people in France and owns several subsidiary companies in other countries, including the Morilla Company in South Madley, Massachusetts.

Frachon himself discovered the modern hot air balloon in 1970 when balloonist and balloon manufacturer Don Cameron organized a balloon flight from Vidalon, carrying Jean-Paul's father, Xavier. Several years later, in 1976, Jean-Paul Frachon and other descendants of the Montgolfier family founded an association and bought their first balloon, which they named *1783*. Soon after that, Frachon acquired his pilot's license.

"What I like about ballooning," Frachon said, "is to be able to fly above the trees and houses, feeling the sensation of freedom and the unexpected, appreciating the beauty and charm of these bright colored globes in the sky or in the fields.

Jean-Paul Frachon in 18th century costume at the 1983 bicentennial celebration of the birth of ballooning, at Annonay, France.

I also enjoy being with the people I meet during the flights or the landings, and who share the same passion."

As a balloonist as well as a Montgolfier descendent, Frachon hosted Annonay's 1983 bicentennial celebration of the birth of ballooning. There are nine balloons in Annonay, including the balloon the paper mill owns as an advertising medium. "The people of Annonay, the birthplace of ballooning, like to see balloons in the sky of their town," Frachon said.

Here, then, is the Montgolfier family's version of the invention and first flights of the hot air balloon. The translation from the French of Jean-Paul Frachon's contribution is by Anick Hausman.

At the end of 1782, during the siege of Gibraltar, Joseph Montgolfier, spending some time in Avignon with some friends, tried to imagine a way to cross enemy lines. He had been thinking about aerial navigation for a long time. In October of 1777, he had told his friend Doctor Duret about his observations of the upward force on a shirt held above a fire to warm it. In Avignon, eager to experiment right away, he asked his hostess for a piece of taffeta that he used to make a bag. Held above the fire in the fireplace, the bag filled with hot smoke and rose to the ceiling of the room. Immediately after making calculations regarding volume and weight, he wrote to his brother Etienne at the paper mill of Vidalon: "Promptly prepare a provision of taffeta and ropes, and you will see one of the most incredible things in the world."

Skeptical until then, Etienne met with Joseph and their brother, the canon Alexandre Montgolfier, and revised the plans and calcula- tions necessary to obtain the optimum shape of the balloon. They conducted several private experiments, and on June 4, 1783, in front of the local people gathered in Annonay, they conducted the first public experiment with a balloon made of cloth and paper with a volume of about 2,200 cubic meters. The successful experiment was authenticated by a statement of the Assembly sent to the Academy of Sciences in Paris.

Etienne went to Paris and built several balloons with the help of his friend Reveillon, who was a manufacturer of wallpaper. Faithful to his promise to his father never to fly, Etienne experimented in the Reveillon gardens. A first balloon without passengers took off from there on September 12, 1783. The second launching – carrying a duck, a rooster, and a sheep – was attended by the King of France on September 19, in Versailles. Finally, on November 21, 1783, the first aerial voyage with human passengers took place with Pilatre de Rozier and the Marquis d'Arlandes aboard the aerostat, Le Reveillon.

These experiments achieved wide renown, and in December of 1783, King Louis XVI ennobled the father of the inventors, Pierre Montgolfier, and on March 19, 1784, the title of "Royal Manufacturer" was granted to the paper mill of Vidalon.

In the meantime, Joseph, still in Annonay and now a member of the Academy of Lyon, built an enormous 20,000-cubic-meter balloon with the help of the Intendant of Fleusselles. His dream was to fly from Lyon to Paris. On January 19, 1784, Le Fleusselles – severely damaged after having been inflated several times and overloaded with eight passengers aboard (Joseph among them) – could fly for only thirteen minutes before landing brusquely a few hundred meters from its point of departure.

The titles and honors did not compensate for the expenses of all the experiments. Etienne came back to Vidalon in June of 1784 and dedicated himself to running the factory. Joseph, moving from one invention to the next, studied the parachute and the hydraulic ram.

The first experiments with hydrogen aerostats had started with the Robert brothers and Professor Charles shortly after the first hot air experiment at Annonay. They conducted their first, unmanned launch at the Champs-de-Mars in Paris on August 27, 1783. Their first manned ascent, with Charles and a Robert aboard, departed from the Tuileries on December 1, 1783. The so-called rivalry between Charles and the Robert brothers and the Montgolfiers does not seem very credible since Etienne Montgolfier attended the first attempts of the Robert brothers.

After a few spectacular ascensions in France and other countries, the hot air aerostation was practically abandoned until the advent of the modern hot air balloon.

Only a year after the first balloon ascents, a thirteen-year-old boy, Edward Warren, was the first to fly a hot air balloon in the United States, when he flew a paper tethered balloon in Baltimore, Maryland. After that, the *montgolfiere* virtually disappeared until the mid-20th century, because it needed to be several times the size of a gas balloon in order to achieve lift, making the balloon difficult to move and handle. Also, it was dangerous in that the aeronauts continually had to feed the fire, spreading sparks which could burn the balloon fabric. Although it took hours to inflate, and gas was more expensive than straw and wool, the smaller gas balloon was easier to transport and work with than the *montgolfiere* and was able to remain aloft for longer periods of time. Of the two kinds of balloons, the gas balloon at that time clearly had the greater number of advantages.

When Benjamin Frankin witnessed the flight of one of Professor Charles's balloons in Paris, another spectator asked him, "What good is it?" Franklin's famous answer was another question: "What good is a newborn baby?" The development of the military, scientific, entertainment, and sporting potential of the gas balloon throughout the 19th century and into the 20th answered the French spectator's question.

Ed Yost

The Development of the Modern Hot Air Balloon

The modern hot air balloon, like the first *montgolfiere* itself, was originally developed for military purposes.

In 1783, Joseph Montgolfier studied the problem of how the French and the Spanish could besiege the British on the rock of Gibralter and concluded that if they could not penetrate the defenses either by land or by sea, perhaps they could by air. It was at this point – supposedly recalling his observation of a shirt or chemise billowing from a fireplace mantel – that he is believed to have envisioned what would become the hot air balloon. For another century and a half, others developed the uses of balloons in warfare. Gas balloons were used for military surveillance by Napoleon and by both the North and the South in the American Civil War. They carried refugees and mail from Paris during the Prussians' Siege of Paris in 1870-1871. Bombs were dropped from them during the 1912 Italo-Turkish War in Tripoli. Both balloons and their airship relatives had many uses during the World Wars, including training and observation.

Ed Yost, regarded as the "Father of Modern Hot Air Ballooning," was first a U.S. Army pilot, then a bush pilot in Alaska before he began working with balloons in the early 1950s for the Office of Naval Research through the Aeronautical Research Division of General Mills. Through General Mills, he was involved with sending leaflets by polyethelene balloons behind the Iron Curtain, and he began researching an alternative to expensive helium used in pilot training balloons.

When General Mills withdrew from ballooning, Yost and others founded Raven Industries, whose hot air balloon division is now Aerostar. A grant from the Office of Naval Research gave Yost the opportunity to develop the envelope and burner system which evolved into the modern hot air balloon, with rip-stop nylon envelope and propane fuel system. He made the first modern hot air balloon flight October 10, 1960, from Bruning, Nebraska. In 1961, Raven hired Don Piccard to promote hot air ballooning, and two years later the two men were the first to cross the English Channel in a hot air balloon.

The Yost-Piccard Channel crossing was the modern hot air equivalent of the Jean Pierre Blanchard and Dr. John Jeffries gas balloon flight of January 7, 1785. Blanchard's balloon, equipped with useless oars and rudder, flew from England to France in two and a half hours, the first balloon crossing of the Channel. During the flight, Blanchard and Jeffries used all their ballast and even had to remove their clothes to keep the balloon airborne. (Only months after the Blanchard crossing, Pilatre de Rozier, the first man to fly, became the first aeronaut to die while ballooning, when his combined hot air and hydrogen balloon exploded in mid-air during an attempted flight from France to England.) Yost and Piccard, flying their hot air balloon, *Channel Champ*, at around 13,000 feet, made their crossing in three hours and seventeen minutes.

In 1973, Yost built a special hot air balloon for a crossing of a different kind: a coast-to-coast voyage across the United States. For millionaire publisher and balloonist Malcolm Forbes, Yost constructed the *Chateau de Balleroy*, a standard-shaped balloon named after Forbes's chateau in France. The balloon – with a special inner coating of aluminized fabric to retain heat – carried Forbes from Coos Bay, Oregon, to Gwynn Island, Virginia, in twenty-one flights in as many days, the first transcontinental crossing in a single hot air balloon.

A few years later, Yost returned to experimenting with gas balloons. He started his own balloon company, Universal Systems, where he developed four gas balloons to cross the Atlantic. His own 1976

Ed Yost in his Skypower gas balloon workshop, near Taos, New Mexico.

solo attempt, in *Silver Fox*, covered 2,474 miles in four-and-a-half days before a southerly trajectory dictated an ocean landing about 700 miles from Portugal. (See *National Geographic*, February 1977.) Yost's fourth Atlantic balloon, *Double Eagle II*, carried Maxie Anderson, Ben Abruzzo, and Larry Newman safely across to France and into the history books. Over the last decades, Yost has also created a fabric sculpture for the National Gallery of Scotland, in Edinburgh, and has been involved with Hollywood, flying his balloons in several films, including *The Great Race, The Great Bank Robbery, Skiddoo,* and *Ragtime.*

Yost and his wife Suzanne now live in the mountains of New Mexico on their Skypower property, where he makes helium balloons in a workshop at the edge of a balloon launch field. During an interview in the workshop, the craggy inventor and adventurer, smoking pipefuls of Prince Albert, paged through his scrapbook of balloon papers and articles spanning nearly forty years.

I started in ballooning about 1950. After World War II, all the scientific people in the U.S. wanted to study primarily cosmic rays, but also wanted to do experiments in the stratosphere. The only way you can get to that altitude where the air density is very thin is to make a balloon envelope extremely large and very light in weight. So the Aeronautical Research Division of General Mills sprang up because General Mills had experience in plastic and packaging. In the beginning, a lot of this stuff was classified, and a lot still is. It turned out, for example, that many of the "flying saucers" sighted in those days were balloons.

I did weather studies for the Office of Naval Research and the Air Force through General Mills. We were working up to about 100,000 feet at that time, with larger and larger balloons. Did all kinds of crazy stuff, like flying leaflets across the Iron Curtain in Europe. Those balloons had a container of dry ice on board. When the dry ice evaporated to a certain point, the thing would turn upside down and dump the payload. People sometimes ask me if the leaflets had any effect. Sure they did. They helped start the Hungarian Revolution.

The helium we were using in balloon pilot training was very expensive, and besides, I was real inquisitive, so in 1955, I started experimenting with hot air balloons. No one else was messing around with hot air systems at that time, but I'd been working with balloons, so it was natural for me to begin playing with that stuff. I inflated my first one with a vacuum cleaner, stuck a plumber's firepot in the end, and got forty pounds of gross lift. We made a thirty-footer which had 16,000 cubic feet of volume. I clustered three of these firepots at the bottom, and that flew the whole thing. I figured then that if I made a thirty-nine-footer with about 27,000 cubic feet of volume, I could fly a man. Which I did. I clustered five firepots and put a man on the line. At the end of the flight, there was no way to get the air out, so we had to squeeze it out. Because of that project, the Office of Naval Research gave me a grant of $47,000. General Mills was getting out of the business, so several of us moved the whole program to South Dakota and started Raven Industries.

At Raven, I was able to make the Naval Research grant last five years because the project entailed mostly investigation of burner techniques, fuel consumption, and envelope materials. I made kerosene burners, one that burned gasoline. We had to pressurize these fuels using a foot pump with a long lever, and you had to just keep pumping pressure into it. You could get mighty tired of that, so we started looking for something else. As for envelopes, there were no fabrics available then like there are now. On one of ours, we laminated a thin layer of mylar inside another fabric.

That was perfect for about five flights – before it de-laminated and all the mylar fell off.

Our first balloon was not a hot air balloon. It was a hot gas balloon because it had combustion gases mixed with air. Nobody could tell what the shape of the balloon should be. I made a balloon that had all kinds of excess material in it. We put the burner on the envelope, added weights to reach 450 pounds gross, and inflated the thing in the Hippodrome at the Minnesota State Fair Grounds.

You had to know the heat values of various fuels. Liquid hydrogen is wow! Then you had to know the temperature profile – how hot it was and if it was going to burn through the skin of the balloon. We inflated that same balloon again, this time with thermistors all over it so we could check the temperatures on both the outside and the inside to know what the temperatures were so we wouldn't burn the top out and kill ourselves. In our first balloons – when we didn't know how hot the things were going to get – the whole bottom was glass cloth, but after we learned what temperature the heat could reach, we returned to fabric, knowing the temperature wouldn't bother it.

After we made a couple of flights, we wanted to know what happens if the fire goes out. We put a radio transmitter on board a fully loaded balloon and arranged for the fuel to burn out in just thirty minutes. With our transmitter, we could tell the altitude, etc. We learned about climb, fuel exhaustion, and descent rate, which was about 1,100 feet a minute, better than a parachute. I put a drag skirt on one, slowing its descent to about 420 feet a minute.

The first flight of our hot air balloon – from Bruning, Nebraska, October 10, 1960 – was pretty miserable. Inside the Hippodrome, it had worked beautifully, but at Bruning, I was burning vapor propane off the top, and it wouldn't vaporize fast enough in the tank to keep me airborne. I was shaking the tanks and everything. On the second flight – a month later, in Rapid City – we used liquid propane from the bottom of the tank, went up around 9,000 feet, and had no problem.

These first two flights had one needle valve to control the fuel to the burner. It took twenty-seven turns to open it and twenty-seven turns to close it. You kept changing the setting so much that when you landed, your arm was so darned tired you couldn't hold it up. So, later, we put two valves in parallel, the needle plus a quick valve so it could override it.

Our burner for liquid propane consisted of a double-walled steel pipe welded top and bottom to form a vaporizing chamber. The fire through the pipe was hotter than hell, but around the outside was quite cool from ambient air. This gave us uneven expansion, and after a few flights, the whole jacket would break open and fire would shoot out everywhere. Shut off the fuel supply and smack the ground again. We had a lot of excitement before we came up with the coiled steel tubing on the burner. Also, we used oxygen tanks from World War II. There was no relief valve on the things and no way to tell how much fuel you had left on board.

When the Navy released the story of the second flight, they said a funny thing, that hot air ballooning might become a sport.

We did the third manned flight on a cold day to see how the balloon would operate in very cold temperatures. It was five degrees, and we were still using the one-needle-valve burner system. After that, I got a contract to make a two-man system and took that down to Albuquerque to do the test flight. That's about the time – September 1961 – that we hired Don Piccard to see if we could sell these balloons commercially. You couldn't give those things away in the beginning.

A couple of years later, in 1963, Piccard and I crossed the English Channel, which I think was probably the first real breakthrough for hot air ballooning. There was a lot of publicity all over the world. When we took off from England, the lower wind was blowing straight towards London. We had to ascend above 13,000 feet to get a wind to take us across. It was very slow. When we were ready to descend in France, the winds down low were blowing back to the North Sea, and they were strong, twenty-five to thirty miles an hour. If we'd missed that landing, we'd have been in the water.

When asked where *Channel Champ* was now – perhaps in the Smithsonian, along with *Double Eagle II* – Yost kicked an envelope bag under the worktable. "There's the sonofagun," he said, through the pipe in his teeth.

Don Piccard

The Promotion of Hot Air Ballooning

Shortly after the first flights of Ed Yost's prototype of the modern hot air balloon, Yost's company, Raven Industries, hired Don Piccard, a member of a famous ballooning family and an experienced gas balloonist, to help adapt the military model for sport use and to promote the revival of the hot air balloon.

The Piccard family has an important place in the scientific tradition of ballooning, which began when Dr. John Jeffries joined Jean Pierre Blanchard in the first balloon crossing of the English Channel. In that flight, Dr. Jeffries conducted research of air temperatures, barometric pressure, and wind currents. High altitude flights, distance flights, and a tragic flight of exploration to the North Pole followed. In 1862, English meteorologist James Glaisher and balloonist Henry Coxwell rose 30,000 feet before Coxwell, with frozen hands, was able to open the balloon's release valve with his teeth. In 1931, Professor Auguste Piccard and his assistant, Paul Kipfer – in a pressurized gondola under a gas balloon – were the first to ascend into the stratosphere and return safely to earth. Don Piccard's father, Jean (Auguste's twin brother), and his mother, Jeannette, also made an historic balloon flight into the stratosphere.

Don Piccard grew up in the traditional world of gas ballooning, and in an adapted Fu-Gos Japanese bomb balloon, he made in 1947 what is regarded as the first free flight after World War II.

Official U.S. Navy photograph

Don Piccard working with gas balloons for the United States Navy during World War II.

Associated with many areas of gas ballooning and later instrumental both in persuading gas balloonists to take hot air balloons seriously and in making the public aware of hot air ballooning, Don Piccard was an important figure in the transition from one kind of aerostation to the other.

In 1962, Piccard organized the first sporting event for modern hot air balloons, the St. Paul Winter Carnival Balloon Race. And the next year was even a more important year for both Don Piccard and hot air ballooning. In 1963, Piccard organized both the second St. Paul Winter Carnival Balloon Race and the first Hot Air Balloon Championship. The championship event was reputed to be the first of its kind to be held for either hot air or gas balloons. That same year, Piccard and Ed Yost were the first to cross the English Channel in a hot air balloon.

Along with Raven and Barnes, Piccard's own company was one of the first manufacturers of hot air balloons, and his were the first modern hot air balloons to appear in Europe. Several of his balloons were purchased in England, helping to establish the sport there.

Speaking from his home in Minneapolis, Don Piccard traced his family's experience with ballooning through three generations. His reminiscences begin with reference to gas ballooning shortly before the turn of the century:

My grandfather on my father's side was the head of the chemistry department at the University of Basel, in Switzerland. When Spelterini, a well-known Swiss aeronaut, made a flight in town, my grandfather took the young twins to see it. They were naturally very interested, as any red-blooded Swiss boys would be. The father then helped them construct a working toy model of the balloon. When they inflated it, it was windy, but my grandfather, being an aggressive professor, wanted to fly it, and the wind destroyed the balloon on its first launch.

Later, the two boys – my father, Jean, and my uncle, Auguste – joined the Swiss Aero Club and did some balloon flying, Auguste more than Jean. During World War I, they were too underweight and tall for the Swiss Army, so they joined the Swiss Army Balloon Observation Corps and were on duty at the border, watching the Germans and the French. After that, while my father was in America raising our family, Auguste was a physics professor at the University of Brussels, doing high altitude research on cosmic rays. This led him back to ballooning and to an invention he and Jean had once come up with. When they were young, an aunt gave them a copy of Jules Verne's Twenty Thousand Leagues Under the Sea. (My brother Paul still has that very book.) The book inspired them to wonder just how deep a submarine could go. They did basic calculations and realized that after you go down a couple thousand feet, the steel walls have to be so strong that it is no longer a buoyant vessel. They came up with the idea of using a lighter-than-water fluid, such as fresh water in the sea and olive oil in fresh water, a buoyancy medium. In effect – back in 1905 – they invented the bathyscaph. They couldn't make it, though, because even then they realized the pressure would be so great that even fused quartz wouldn't be strong enough for windows. The actual bathyscaph was not made until after World War II, but my uncle created the stratospheric version of it to carry physicists up ten miles into the air.

That's what Auguste used on his 1931 flight from Augsburg, Germany, man's first flight into physiological space. The winch operating the valve to let gas out of the balloon to make it come down had been fouled by an unauthorized rope that one of the German ground handlers had put on to help hold the balloon after the aeronauts were already sealed into the cabin. After the sun set and their hydrogen cooled and contracted, they finally landed out of control on a glacier in the Bavarian Alps.

They were colder than Billy Ned on that first flight, so for the second flight, Auguste painted half of the sphere white and half of it black so he could rotate it toward the sun and away from the sun. But on that second flight, the rotating mechanism didn't work. They were able, though, to get the measurements from when the black was toward the sun and when the white side was toward the sun – mathematical calculations that later turned out to be accurate for balloons flying at those altitudes. (Mother used to say, "It's nice to have a cool head and warm feet rather than cold feet and a hot head.") Another thing, their cabin was dented before the flight, so there was a hole in the bottom of the gondola where an instrument was supposed to be. So, after they launched and were ascending rapidly, they had no way to valve gas out of the balloon and couldn't make the gondola cabin airtight. With some oakum and Vaseline, Auguste plugged up the hole, and away they went. If they'd been considerably higher, they might not have gotten back down to the tropopause before the sun would hit them in the morning and take them up again. There were a lot of things on those flights that were very fortunate. Their balloon design had a lot of built-in safety features, so even in spite of their mishaps, they still survived.

At that time, during the Depression, my father lost his organic chemical research job and he felt like retiring to a chicken farm, but my mother would have no part of that. Instead, they pursued getting sponsorship to make a stratospheric flight in this country. That got my mother interested in learning to fly. Back in 1934, anybody sort of wondered about a woman who wanted to fly balloons, but Ed Hill – who was a winner of the Gordon Bennett Balloon Race and was a glider enthusiast and balloonist in the Detroit area – began giving her flight lessons. Her first flight was a special one for her. Ed began descending towards an apple orchard in full bloom. A few moments before the basket would be augering into the ground, Ed throws some ballast out of the back side. The balloon slows its descent and brushes through the tops of the apple trees. The balloon keeps going, the basket hangs back a moment, and then swings forward, and the balloon goes up again. Ed Hill is leaning back in the swinging basket, an apple blossom twig hanging over his right ear. Apple blossom petals are strewn over everything. His eyes are bright, and he's smiling and laughing because he has seen by the expression on Jeannette's face that she loved it. She wasn't a terrified woman. She was a balloon pilot in the making. It was her coming back and telling that story to the rest of the family that inspired me, at the age of eight, to get into ballooning.

Later that year, on October 23, she and my father made their stratospheric flight, launching from Ford Airport, in Dearborn, Michigan, and landing in Cadiz, Ohio. They reached 57,579 feet, nearly eleven miles, the highest any woman had piloted any aircraft in history, and she held that distinction for about fifty years.

It was while I was in the Navy during World War II that I first got involved with the actual flying of balloons. I made two dozen helium balloon flights out of Lakehurst, New Jersey, where the Hindenburg disaster had occurred back in 1937. After the war, I took a little war souvenir back to Minnesota with me, a Japanese mulberry-paper bomb balloon, one of those the Japanese sent on wind currents over the Pacific. I designed and built a valve for it, built a basket, developed a new rigging and inflation system, and made my first solo balloon flight in February 1947. Using hydrogen, I flew out of downtown Minneapolis and landed two hours later near White Bear Lake, at St. Paul. Interesting flight, cold weather. At the edge of one frozen lake, I told a fellow to grab the drag rope, and I pulled him across the ice, doing what I call balloonjoring. That flight earned me my FAA Commercial Balloon Pilot's license.

A few years later, I started the Balloon Club of America with my old $10 Navy surplus balloon and got several old Army balloons free. Mike Todd rented one of them from us, painted it up as La Coquette, and featured it in his film, Around the World in 80 Days. Even though there wasn't a balloon in the novel, it really was the spirit of the movie and did a great deal to popularize the sport of ballooning.

That group of ours would meet Friday evenings in Swarthmore, Pennsylvania, and if the weather looked good after our meeting, we'd go down to the barn, load up the balloon stuff, haul it to Conshohocken or Valley Forge, unload it, fill the sandbags, spread out the balloon, spread out the net, hook it up, and by about two or three in the morning, we'd be ready to start inflating with gas. The gas company would show up, connect the pipe, and spend the next three or four hours putting gas into the balloon. We'd use 128 sandbags around the balloon, each one weighing thirty-five pounds. Raw hands, gas smell, wet because the dew is falling on everything – just not a real enjoyable way to spend a Friday night. So finally, at dawn, the balloon would be full and we'd take off, half of us would fall asleep, and we'd land over in New Jersey someplace. It was a great sport. The club really helped establish the sport of ballooning again in the post-war era. It was probably more of a fun social sport than it had been before, when it was more of a competitive thing.

After returning to Minnesota, I began working for the G.T. Schjeldahl Company, which was making mylar balloons for high altitude research. I set the first world class A-1 altitude record in one, got good press, and it enticed other people to break the record and get press for themselves and for ballooning. That happened with several records I set temporarily. We got a lot of interest in the sport through records and record-breaking.

I was happy the records got publicity because I saw ballooning as a fun sport, exciting, interesting, and yet poetic and beautiful at the same time. It's also a team sport, with the family participating. Women and children can become pilots, too. You can just go out and fly around for the day and have fun.

Most people at that time, though, still looked on ballooning as an oddity. Wally Scholl, an old carnival balloonist, said that when you'd check into a hotel, they would send the bellboy up to take the sheets off the bed before they'd let you into the room. First of all, they thought you'd ruin the sheets with all the soot that was all over you, and secondly, if you didn't ruin them, you'd steal them to repair your balloon. After the Wright Brothers, ballooning became the bastard side of aviation.

While I was still engaged with gas ballooning, working to make it accepted, General Mills had a government contract for developing hot air balloons. Then Raven Industries got the contract and developed a one-man hot air balloon that was a little bosun's chair with a couple of lightweight steel tanks, and an envelope forty feet in diameter. It worked very well. Raven hired me to get some publicity for hot air ballooning as a sport. I was able to make a lot of changes in the system, and we soon had a vehicle that could be sold.

At the St. Paul Winter Carnival in 1962, I convinced John Geisler, the executive director, to let us have a balloon race. The first thing I did to try to give hot air ballooning credibility was use the funds of private sponsors to purchase a twelve-inch sterling silver trophy which had the sophistication of trophies awarded at yacht races and horse shows. That was one of the things that helped the press see ballooning as a class sport rather than a carnival gimmick.

Another early advancement for hot air ballooning evolved from a letter I wrote to an old friend, the well-known French balloonist Charles Dollfus, telling him how the Raven hot air balloon was coming along. Charles wrote back saying that if the hot air balloon could do everything I said it could, it was time to fly it across the English Channel. That's the great test. If you want to prove that the time for any new invention has come, you have to cross the Channel with it. As it worked out, Ed Yost and I did it. The flight was a very dramatic thing which made international publicity. It was the coming of age for the sport of hot air ballooning.

In 1964, Raven temporarily closed down their sport balloon business, so I went out to California and started my own.

I've been ballooning most of my life. I've flown mylar, polyethelene, nylon, cotton, and paper balloons, with hydrogen, helium, coal gas, natural gas, and hot air, but what I love most about ballooning is the interrelation of motion. Flying with a group of balloons at Albuquerque, say, is so much more fun than just flying out by yourself in the country because you have the interrelation of movement between you and the other balloons. Flying in the middle of those balloons in the "Albuquerque Box," with those above you going north and those below you going south, everything moving, is such a poetic and incomprehensible thing.

While Don Piccard was working to gain popular acceptance of the hot air balloon, Tracy Barnes began his balloon manufacturing company, developed the balloon deflation top and other systems and in 1966 made the first hot air balloon crossing of the United States, flying two different balloons over a five-month period. American balloon manufacturers grew throughout the 1960s, and the hot air balloon continued to evolve.

Sid Cutter
The Albuquerque International Balloon Fiesta

By the early 1970s, the hot air balloon was ready for the attention and cameras of the general public. In 1971, Sid Cutter held a balloon event which within a few years would evolve into the largest international gathering of hot air balloons in the world. Gas ballooning had the Gordon Bennett International Balloon Race, a highly publicized long-distance race begun in 1906 and continuing up to 1938 and the outbreak of World War II. Hot air ballooning has the Albuquerque International Hot Air Balloon Fiesta, which each year draws hundreds of balloons and pilots from more than thirty countries around the world.

With its sheer magnitude and color, the Albuquerque Fiesta has popularized the sport as no other event has, becoming identified with hot air ballooning itself in the eyes of the public. The Fiesta's influence has also been felt in a more subtle way by balloonists themselves. Born into a famous aviation family of the Southwestern United States, Sid Cutter was able to change the condescension of airplane pilots toward hot air ballooning to acceptance of the sport, just as Don Piccard had earlier helped make hot air ballooning respectable in the eyes of gas balloonists.

In the 1970s, when the Albuquerque Fiesta was growing in size year by year, American balloon manufacturers were joined by British companies and a few French companies. Don Cameron's

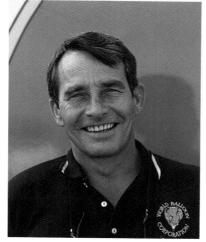

Sid Cutter beside one of his World Balloon Corporation vehicles on the hot air balloon meet circuit.

Cameron Balloons became the dominant European balloon company and now produces special-shape balloons seen at most balloon festivals. Another manufacturer of special shapes is Thunder and Colt. Per Lindstrand, director of Thunder and Colt, teamed up with Richard Branson in 1987 to be the first to cross the Atlantic in a specially constructed hot air balloon.

There are now about 5,000 United States balloon pilots licensed by the Federal Aviation Administration, and 3,000 balloons. And the size of ballooning brings with it an interest in its past. Malcolm Forbes established the first balloon museum, at his Normandy chateau. The permanent National Balloon Museum, in Indianola,

Iowa, officially opened in 1988. It houses a collection of balloon memorabilia belonging to the Balloon Federation of America. The Maxie Anderson-Ben Abruzzo International Balloon Museum, in Albuquerque, is in the final planning stage.

Cutter – a veteran aviator with 20,000 hours of general aviation and Air Force flying time and 4,000 hours of balloon flying – is a two-time national hot air balloon champion. After several years of working in both aviation and ballooning, he eventually chose ballooning. Behind his cluttered desk at the World Balloon Corporation, in Albuquerque, he told his own special version of his initiation to hot air ballooning, an initiation which eventually led to the Albuquerque International Hot Air Balloon Fiesta.

I grew up in aviation. My dad started his business in 1928. The way I got into ballooning was through a party we decided to have for all our customers to celebrate forty-two years of being in business. At the same time, it happened to be a birthday party for my mother. We made it on the World War I theme, with Snoopy and the Red Baron, and decided to have it in a hangar because we couldn't afford a hall.

We ordered a lot of First World War German, British, and French uniforms out of California, and we'd have five different bars going in the hangar with all these guys dressed up in old military uniforms. My brother Bill and I chose to be Snoopy and the Red Baron. I wanted to decorate the hangar with some old-time airplanes, but they're so delicate and hard to come by that I finally stumbled on the idea of putting a balloon in there. They had balloons in WWI. I contacted the FAA, and they said, oh sure, there were balloons around – and there were, but very few in those days.

I thought I might be able to rent one around here. I found out that a guy in Tucson wanted $500 for the day, plus expenses. I asked him how much it would cost to buy a balloon. He said $5,000. I decided I would just buy one and tie it up for advertising outside.

15

I didn't know what made balloons work, and I didn't know how big they were, or anything.

I looked up balloon manufacturers in Dun and Bradstreet. Raven was the only one listed, so I gave them a call. They sent me some literature which described two different-sized models, and they were just coming out with a third. I called them again and said, "I'm having this party in ten days. Can you send me your Model 50 by then?" Their rep said they could make the balloon in ten days, but that they wouldn't be able to get it out to me in that time. I said that was all right, I'd fly out and pick it up and they could show me how to inflate it. The rep said I probably couldn't get the gondola into the airplane. I asked him if the gondola was already made, and he said it was. I told him to ship the gondola to me and I'd pick up the envelope. One of their ladies made me the envelope in ten days. I flew up through a bunch of tornadoes, and they showed me how to inflate the balloon. When I saw it inflated, I didn't know if it would fit in the hangar.

We made it fit. At the party that night, I had Those Magnificent Men in Their Flying Machines *showing in one corner of the hangar, and on the buffet table I had an ice carving of Snoopy and the Red Baron. The balloon was all squished down because it was too big for the hangar, but even so, it was still the hit of the evening.*

My brother kept telling everyone we were going to fly in it the next day, and I kept telling him I didn't know anything about balloons. It was a great party, finally breaking up around two the next morning.

At 6 a.m., my mother and brother showed up at my house with the balloon all packed up, ready to go flying. Now, legally we could fly it, because we all had balloon licenses, even my mother. At that time, all you needed for a balloon license was a flight physical, and they would write you out a license for hot air balloons only. The license was a great conversation piece at parties. So, we did have a legal license to pilot a balloon, but there was no one around to teach us how to fly the darned thing.

"Bill," I said, trying to get out of it, "we don't have any fuel."

"Oh yes we do," he said. "I got some on the way home."

We drove out to the International Airport and inflated and tethered the balloon right there. I took my mother up on a tethered "flight," came back down, let her out, and Bill climbed in. I was planning to take him up and come back down, and then we would all go out to breakfast.

There must have some miscommunication, because when the balloon reached the end of the rope, they let the rope go, and we started heading right toward some power lines. Balloons didn't have a lot of power in those days, and I didn't really know what we were doing, so I decided we were going to fly.

My brother was pulling up the rope like mad so it wouldn't hit the power lines, and I took the balloon up to about 300 feet, scared to go any higher because I didn't know how long the fuel was supposed to last, and I couldn't go any lower because of the power line right under us. It was one of those perfect days for ballooning, or I wouldn't be doing it today.

For an hour, we flew right along with that power line. I'll say that flying real low, at 300 feet, it looked like nothing but telephone poles, and when you don't know when your fuel's going to run out, it's scary. When I fly now, I sit up on the side of the gondola and it doesn't bother me, but then I was sitting on the propane tank with my nose on the edge of the gondola, pulling on the burner chain.

We finally drifted away from the power line. We had a little radio with us, so I called on it and had them call my wife to tell her to go to the door and look south, because we were heading her way. As it turned out, we landed in a little hollow a block and a half from my house. We lost the chase crew because they couldn't see us down in there, so I walked home.

No one was there. I called the airport, got my mother, said the balloon was close to home, and I wondered where my wife and daughter were. My mother said they were there at the airport. I asked what they were doing there. She said, "Here, you talk to them," and gave my wife the phone. I asked her what she was doing at the airport.

"We got so excited that we came here to see you land," she said.

"The balloon is a block and a half away from the house," I said.

"But you always land at the airport," she said.

People just didn't know much about ballooning in those days.

After that, it became common knowledge around Albuquerque that I had a balloon. A local radio and television station was going to have its 50th anniversary and celebrate it with a giant birthday cake, and they wondered if they could talk me into having a balloon ascension. I said I knew of two or three other balloons and that maybe we could have a balloon race. I called a balloonist to find out what a balloon race was and found out that one balloon takes off, everyone chases it, and whoever gets the closest to it wins the race. People at the station asked what the biggest balloon race in the world was. I'd read that there were once nineteen balloons at a meet in England. They asked if I could get twenty-one. I didn't know if there were that many balloon pilots in all of America. I was finally able to contact twenty-one pilots, but just before the meet there was a snowstorm in Chicago, so we ended up with fourteen balloons here. Albuquerque was ready for it. When the balloonists gathered at the field at 6 a.m., there were 30,000 people there.

One person at the race that day, Don Kersten, had just returned from the Federation Aeronautique Internationale meeting in Paris and had been given authority to hold the first World Hot Air Balloon Championship. The city of Albuquerque had been looking for something to hang its hat on. They had tried chile cook-offs and things of that sort, but a balloon fiesta looked like something really special. So, we made a bid for the first World Championship, and got it. I didn't know at the time that nobody else wanted it. To have a real spectacular event, we invited the national champion, Bruce Comstock, and other well-known competitors. We ended up with 138 balloons from seventeen countries.

When we held the second World Championship here, in 1975, with 168 balloons, the city began to think about taking it over. I still ran it, but they started paying the bills. What they did was put together a non-profit corporation of interested citizens, got a little pump-priming from some people to get it started, and slowly built it up from there. You can't do it as private enterprise, because you have to pay so many people. It'll work only as a non-profit deal, because that way you can get hundreds of volunteers.

What I wanted – no matter how it could be handled – was something for the city, a festival, and balloons are so natural for that. Everybody loves a balloon.

For balloonists, ballooning is a social sport. There's a lot of camaraderie involved. It takes three or four people anyway, and if you have twenty-four people, it's that much more fun. Everybody can join in: the dogs, the grandparents, the toddlers. And for everybody else, it makes them happy just to see a balloon. It's the gaiety of color. Balloons have every color of the rainbow, and every balloon is different. They really create an impression. And there's the romance to them, a certain mystique about somebody going up in them. Now, you can tether a balloon to draw attention, but if it doesn't fly away, people start wondering why. When people see a balloon flying with people in it, it really stimulates the imagination. For me, one of the most rewarding ballooning experiences I've ever had is landing in a school yard. Those little faces just shine, as though they've seen a miracle. And as far as I'm concerned, they have.

I keep trying to get the city to expand the Fiesta and pick up other interest groups with other activities, like an airshow, a model airplane contest, equestrian shows, parades. I have proposed a 1,000-balloon race, not launching them from one place but from all over town, in groups of 100, giving all of them the signal simultaneously by shooting off a cannon. Just imagine it, 1,000 balloons rising at the same time, painting the sky with color!

• Winds up to about twelve miles an hour are suitable for flying. A typical hot air balloon flight lasts between one and two hours.

• A hot air balloon ascends with blasts of heat from the burners. A balloon descends slowly with the cooling of air inside the envelope, or more quickly with the release of air from the **maneuvering vent**. The vent is either in the side of the envelope, or up at the **crown** of the envelope, near the **deflation panel**. A balloon's course being determined by the wind, a balloon can be "steered" only by the pilot ascending or descending to a wind blowing in a different direction.

The Modern Hot Air Balloon

• The standard hot air balloon **envelope**, constructed of synthetic materials, ranges in size from 50,000 to 85,000 cubic feet. A **skirt** is attached to the **mouth**, or **throat**, of the envelope.

• The typical balloon **basket**, or **gondola**, holds either three ten-gallon tanks of propane gas or two twenty-gallon tanks and can carry up to four passengers.

• A double **burner** system generates 24 million BTUs per hour.

Albuquerque Balloon Fiesta
Ed Dosien

The Great Balloon Festival

Imagine a great balloon festival, with more than 1,000 balloons rising across North America and flying over desert, plains, farmland, lakes, forests, mountains – from Calgary to Atlanta, Sacramento to Montreal. An entire ballooning season is here condensed into a single balloon festival beginning with the arrival of balloonists, continuing through the daybreak launch of balloons across the United States and Canada, and ending in the evening with a serene Balloon Glow.

19

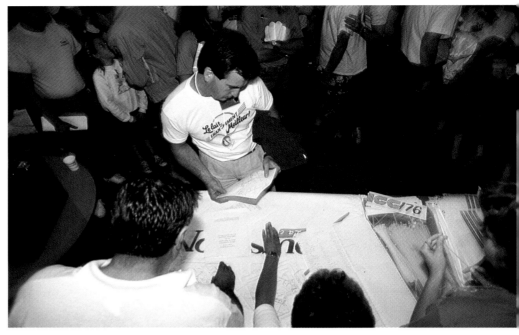

Pilot registration.

Balloonists

"For me, there's no more fun in the world than flying a balloon. I'm a nut for balloons."   *(Balloonist)*

After a year of planning for their balloon festivals, cities and towns across North America are ready for the arrival of the hot air balloon pilots and crews the afternoon before the big launch. Store windows are bright with painted balloons, business signs declare, "Welcome, Ballooners," and hotel clerks are eager to begin collecting balloon pins.

Balloon vehicles appear on the streets – colorfully painted vans, trailers, and pick-up trucks which hold the promise of the romance and adventure stuffed in the balloon envelope bags in the back of the vehicles. Balloonists' customized license plates are footnotes of individuality.

At pilot registration, trading a logbook check for pilot packs, the balloonists reveal themselves in their true colors, their dress ranging from corporate pilot uniforms to caps and vests covered with balloon pins, to outrageous balloon-shaped hats or jump suits made of balloon-print material. Jackets announce "Rainbow Rider," praise "Ballooning, the Gentle Adventure." Tee-shirt names and logos evoke festivals past, from France to Japan. There are also pilots in workshoes and blue jeans, with leather gloves sticking out of their back pockets.

Call them aeronauts, sky-sailors, balloonists, ballooners, balloonatics. They come from all backgrounds – aeronautics, farming, academia, the business world – and they're all involved in ballooning to different degrees. Some own balloon manufacturing companies; some drive 50,000 miles a year as corporate pilots; some

Holiday Inn®
SHELL
WELCOME
BALLOONISTS
CREWS AND
SPECTATORS

Opposite page:
Balloonists and mascot. Below,
typical high spirits of pilots and
crews.

The owner of this customized
license plate originally had a
plate spelled, "Baloner," but he
changed the spelling after
many people asked him what a
"Baloner" was.

Balloon pins and patches –
standard balloonist equipment.

operate their own balloon businesses by
offering champagne flights, tethered rides,
flight instruction, hot- and cold-air balloon
advertising; some compete as a hobby; some
just fly when they can for the sheer fun of it.
Many make ballooning a family affair, with the
spouse as crew chief and children as crew.

Whatever the background and whatever the
involvement, they are balloonists because, at
some point, they came under the spell of a
hot air balloon. Often, that moment was when
they first saw a balloon. One balloonist-to-be
first saw an envelope deflated on the ground
and followed the chase vehicle on his bike.
Another, older, was flying a glider when he
passed the first balloon he'd ever seen and
knew right then that after he landed he would
begin looking for a balloon to buy.

Others, inspired by pictures of balloons,
made miniature aerostats out of plastic bags
and found a way to heat the air inside them,
making them fly. One young lady took a
ballooning course in college, fell in love with
both ballooning and the instructor, married the
instructor and got a pilot's license. After her
first balloon ride, another pilot "was floating
at a thousand feet for three days." Becoming
enamored of ballooning is so common that
balloonists have a saying for it (the numbers
changing to reflect current balloon-ride and
balloon prices): "Your first ride costs you
$150. Your second costs you $15,000."

After pilot registration, the pilots and crews
gather for a balloonists' reception, hosted by
sponsors, a Chamber of Commerce, or a
balloon company handling the meet. After the
food and drink and the inevitable ballooning
stories, the doings break up at a respectable
hour. Balloonists' alarm clocks ring early. ■

Atlanta Balloon Festival
Ed Dosien

Senators' Classic
Ed Dosien

Pages 24 and 25:
Members of an Iowa county
cattlemen's association grill up
a hamburger feast for farmers
and balloonists at a landowners
appreciation barbecue.

U.S. National Balloon Championship
Ed Dosien

Opposite page, top:
After a pilot briefing and a
Balloonmeister's decision to
launch, a costumed crew
prepares to drive to the launch
field.

Sacramento Balloon Festival
Ed Dosien

Pilot Briefing

Leaving a briefing, a pilot holds a
bright orange beanbag marker in one
hand, a bottle of champagne in the
other. "Well, we're all set," he says.
"We can fly anywhere now."

After the alarms and wake-up calls around 4 a.m., pilots and crews listen for rain or the sound of wind. They look outside, step out onto balconies or outside the motel door and scan the sky for stars or clouds. They watch the movement of flags, hoping cloth will be hanging limp or fluttering, but not streaming or snapping, and they note whether smoke is rising straight up or at an angle. In some areas, the wind is blowing mightily, and in a few it's raining, but even there, the weather may change by scheduled lift-off time – or may be different at the launch site – so it's time to get ready to go to the pilot briefing.

Already out on the road are other balloon vehicles – many with the telltale baskets on trailers – and spectators driving to the site. Balloonists enter the area by their own access road and gather at the briefing center. With coffee, maps, and notebooks, the pilots answer roll call. The Festival Director introduces the Balloonmeister and the other officers responsible for the safety of the launch. The Weather Officer reports on conditions of the last few hours and projected conditions in the area through the scheduled flight window. Readings of the angles and speed of ascent of helium-filled "pibals," pilot balloons, indicate the winds aloft.

At this point, some flights are cancelled,

Festival de Montgolfieres
Ed Dosien

Festival de Montgolfieres
Ed Dosien

Kentucky Derby Balloon Race
Bob Brown

Kodak Balloonfest
Ed Dosien

27

Albuquerque Balloon Fiesta
Ed Dosien

This page and opposite page, top: Awaiting the "go" or "no-go" word of the Balloonmeister.

Senators' Classic
Ed Dosien

Opposite page, bottom: Before a flight, a costumed corporate pilot is interviewed by a local television station. Balloon festivals are a natural feature subject for journalists.

and some are put on hold, with a later briefing scheduled, in hopes the weather will improve. But pilots are patient and philosophical. "It's always better to be on the ground wishing you were in the air than in the air wishing you were on the ground," one pilot says.

Where the launch is a "go," the Balloonmeister explains what competitive "tasks" will be flown as dictated by wind direction. He gives target coordinates, the size of the maximum scoring area, the time of the launch windows. He points out Red Areas on the maps – Prohibited Zones pilots are to avoid landing in – and reviews local agricultural conditions, explaining that it is cotton planting time, or wheat and barley harvest, or that the entire area is extremely dry, demanding special care with burners. Landowner relations are discussed at length, with the Balloonmeister stressing that chase crews must obtain signatures on landowner releases before driving onto private property.

The briefing ends with the Balloonmeister wishing the balloonists a good flight, and the pilots pick up beanbag markers for the competitive events and traditional bottles of champagne on their way out.

At some festivals, pilot briefings are held at a balloonist headquarters, while at other festivals, briefings are held near or even on the launch site. ■

U.S. National Balloon Championship
Ed Dosien

Kentucky Derby Balloon Race
Ed Dosien

29

*Spectators gather in front of an
information board listing
designated balloon positions on
the launch field.*

Albuquerque Balloon Fiesta
Bob Brown

Spectators

"One of the nicest things about balloning is the looks on people's faces." (Balloonist)

Other people are sleeping comfortably on a Saturday morning while balloon festival-goers are out in the dark, driving to a launch site to watch magic happen.

On midways shining in the pre-dawn darkness, music over a PA system creates a feeling of festivity. Spectators line up outside concession trailers, eager for coffee or hot chocolate, a breakfast roll or fried-dough "Elephant Ears."

By the thousands, the hundreds of thousands, they gather around the edges of the launch field, set up lawn chairs on hillsides, spread blankets on the grass, cock their cameras.

Albuquerque Balloon Fiesta
Bob Brown

■　31

U.S. National Balloon Championship
Ed Dosien

Albuquerque Balloon Fiesta
Ed Dosien

U.S. National Balloon Championship
Ed Dosien

U.S. National Balloon Championship
Ed Dosien

U.S. National Balloon Championship
Ed Dosien

Grand Teton Balloon Race
Ed Dosien

Albuquerque Balloon Fiesta
Ed Dosien

Albuquerque Balloon Fiesta
Ed Dosien

Opposite page:
Yawning, rubbing eyes, drinking
coffee, Idaho spectators wait for
a morning launch to get under
way, while thousands gather
for a mass ascension at the
Albuquerque International
Balloon Fiesta.

Laying Out

A pilot opening an envelope bag,
pulling out coiled cables: "Oh
boy, what do we do with all this
stuff?"   *(Pilot humor)*

Balloon vehicles arrive on the field. An announcer greets the crowd, explains the parts of the balloon, the preparation and inflation process, and what makes a balloon work. The vehicles park at their pre-assigned spots, facing upwind.

The eastern sky tinges orange. A burner blasts, and flame streams up into the dark, drawing the attention of the crowd, as a pilot tests propane lines and burners. The sky lightens. A released helium balloon rises, drifting at a slight angle; then higher, smaller, it shrinks away. A pilot sighting through a compass tracks the flight of the balloon, determining any wind change since the pilot briefing.

Meanwhile, out on roads near the launch site, competition pilots are searching for places from which to launch, plotting their maps, releasing toy helium balloons.

Across the launch field, ground crews of three to five people – from inexperienced volunteers to veteran crew members – assemble their balloons. They unload baskets, envelopes, and inflator fans from the chase vehicles, attach uprights and burners. They unwrap envelope cables coiled inside the envelope bags, secure the cables to the uprights. They pick up envelope bags and carry them away from baskets, "walking out" or "laying out" the envelopes. From one end of the launch area to the other, colors stream out of bags across grass or concrete.

While some crew members check matched velcro patches or wire catches securing parachute tops, others carefully spread out the bright fabric, readying it for cold inflation. ■ 35

LAYING OUT

These pages:
Pre-flight assembly of baskets,
uprights, burners, load cables,
and the spreading out of
balloon envelopes.

Conner Prairie Balloon Classic
Bob Brown

Walla Walla Balloon Stampede
Bob Brown

Quechee Balloon Festival
Ed Dosien

Walla Walla Balloon Stampede
Ed Dosien

Senators' Classic
Ed Dosien

Battle Creek Balloon Championship
Ed Dosien

Battle Creek Balloon Championship
Ed Dosien

Above:
A quick stop at concession stands before balloon inflation begins.

Conner Prairie Balloon Classic
Ed Dosien

LAYING OUT

Walla Walla Balloon Stampede
Bob Brown

Calgary Stampede Balloon Race
Bob Brown

Walla Walla Balloon Stampede
Ed Dosien

Some crews spread out ground cloths to protect the fabric envelopes during the laying-out.

38

Walla Walla Balloon Stampede
Ed Dosien

Walla Walla Balloon Stampede
Bob Brown

Sacramento Balloon Festival
Bob Brown

Walla Walla Balloon Stampede
Ed Dosien

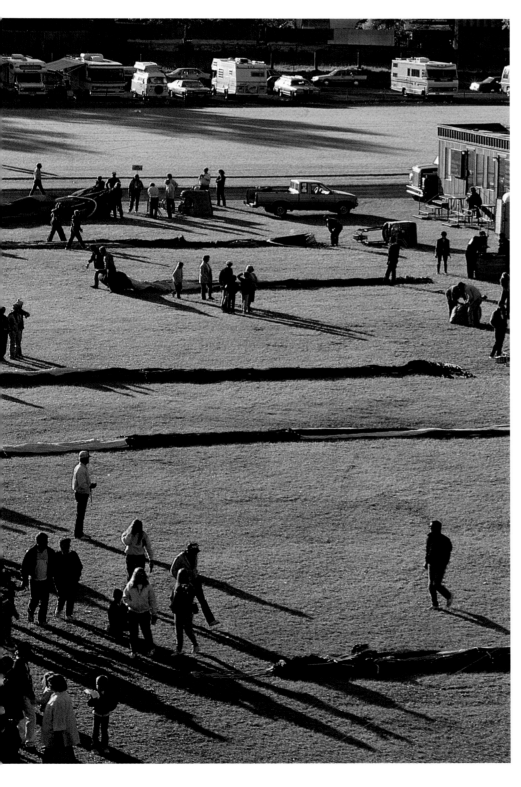

Walla Walla Balloon Stampede
Ed Dosien

LAYING OUT

Pages 40 and 41:
While the rest of the crew is
engaged in pre-flight
preparations, a pilot and crew
chief review the assigned
competitive task of the
morning.

Battle Creek Balloon Championship
Ed Dosien

Walla Walla Balloon Stampede
Bob Brown

Kentucky Derby Balloon Race
Bob Brown

Kodak Balloonfest
Ed Dosien

Page 44:
Conner Prairie Balloon Classic
Ed Dosien

Festival de Montgolfieres
Ed Dosien

Canadian Fantasy Festival
Ed Dosien

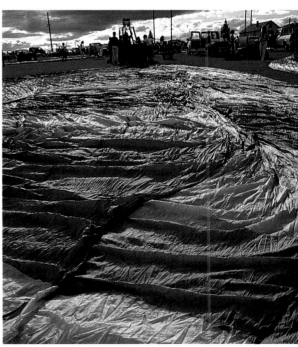

Calgary Stampede Balloon Race
Bob Brown

Conner Prairie Balloon Classic
Ed Dosien

Walla Walla Balloon Stampede
Ed Dosien

Quechee Balloon Festival
Ed Dosien

45

*Pages 44 and 45
and these pages:
While pre-flight preparations
continue at most launch sites of
the Great Balloon Festival, other
sheduled launches are rained out.
At one muddy site, a corporate
balloon is inflated and tethered for
the sake of both the disappointed
spectators and the corporate
sponsor.*

Albuquerque Balloon Fiesta
Ed Dosien

*Two generations of balloonists
at the crown line, controlling
the movement of an inflating
envelope.*

Inflation

*"An inflating balloon is like a giant
heart beginning to beat."* (Balloonist)

The leader, or Hare, balloon lifts off to the clapping and cheering of spectators. Inflator fans across the launch field roar into action like airplane engines, sending currents of excitement through the crowd.

Ground crew members hold open the mouth of their balloon envelope, and the fan is positioned so that air is blowing straight in. What had been a strip of colored fabric upon the launch area now begins to ripple with air. The fabric billows.

"It's alive!" a spectator exclaims, watching the envelope grow, like a giant rising out of the ground.

Inside an inflating envelope, the folds of fabric spread like moving water. A bulge moves from the outside in, the pilot walking under the cloth, suddenly emerging through the maneuvering vent. Without walking on the fabric, the pilot moves inside the expanding cavern of color, straightening deflation and vent lines, examining the envelope, checking to be certain the deflation top is securely fastened.

To a spectator peering inside, into a fantasy of color, the pilot is a miniature figure wandering inside a flower blossom, a kaleidoscope, a stained-glass cathedral. The shadows of crew or spectators outside lengthen and curve through the cloth like spirits from another world.

The pilot reappears beside the gondola – lying on its side, facing the mouth of the basket – and steps inside the uprights. Now that the envelope is filled to about three-

*Opposite page:
Crew members holding
envelope throat open for
inflation in pre-dawn cold.*

*This page:
(Top) Inside the inflating
Flying Saucer balloon.
(Center) Photographing the
inside of an envelope through
the balloon's maneuvering vent.
(Bottom) Guiding the unfolding
fabric.*

quarters' capacity with cold air, it is ready for
the hot-air stage of the inflation. As the pilot
crouches behind the burners, the crew
members holding open the throat lean to the
outside, looking away. The pilot aims the
burner, pulls the valve. Flame blasts into the
envelope. A spectator walking past the basket
jumps, and kids cover their ears.

The envelopes swell, pressing against each
other, until the entire launch field is blooming
with fabric.

When the air inside an envelope is warmer
than the air outside, the balloon begins to rise.
A crew member strains against the crown line
attached to the top of the balloon, controlling
the movement of the balloon, keeping the
envelope from rocking wildly from its own rising. The pilot, hitting the burner with one
hand and holding onto the uprights with the
other, rides the basket up straight. Envelope
after envelope stands, some rubbing others as
they rise, their shapes shifting like soap bubbles, adjusting to the movement.

Spectators venture among the shadowy cloth
canyons of the upright balloons, gather around
the gondolas, and peer up into the fabric
domes shining with color.

Pre-assigned passengers climb into balloon
baskets. A launch official in radio contact with
the Launch Director gives the pilot of a downwind balloon permission to lift off. The pilot
asks passengers and crew if everyone is ready.
They are. The pilot hits the burner, tells the
crew "Hands off," and the balloon rises off the
ground, passengers waving, crowd waving, a
crew member calling out, "Don't forget to

write." ∎

U.S. National Balloon Championship
Ed Dosien

U.S. National Balloon Championshi
Ed Dosie

Kodak Balloonfest
Ed Dosien

This page, top:
The opaque exterior and the
translucent interior of a balloon
envelope, complete with the
shadowy forms of spectators.

Kodak Balloonfe
Ed Dosie

Quechee Balloon Festival
Ed Dosien

U.S. National Balloon Championship
Ed Dosien

A sunrise inflation and a taut
crown line.

This page:
Freeform material and freeform
shadows.

Battle Creek Balloon Championship
Ed Dosien

Deflation tops attached to envelopes with velcro or spring clips. A pilot deflates the balloon by pulling the deflation line, attached to the inside of the crown material.

Battle Creek Balloon Championship
Ed Dosien

Conner Prairie Balloon Classic
Ed Dosien

Canadian Fantasy Festival
Ed Dosien

Quechee Balloon Festival
Ed Dosien

Above:
Pilots inspecting the interiors of
their balloons.

Cold-air inflation. The crown
line of another inflating balloon
bisects the photograph.

Calgary Stampede Balloon Race
Bob Brown

57

INFLATION

This page:
Two views – one from the
crown and one from the throat
of the balloon – of a pilot
inspecting the envelope and
lines during cold inflation.
Pilots enter an inflating balloon
through the maneuvering vent
to avoid walking on the fabric.

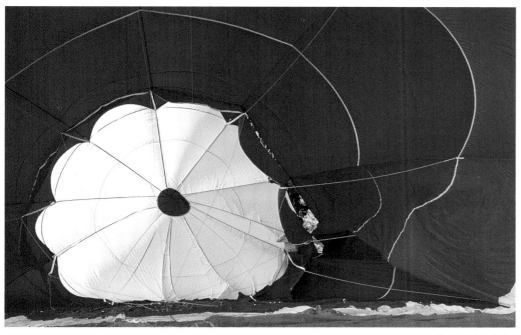

Quechee Balloon Festival
Ed Dosien

Calgary Stampede Balloon Race
Bob Brown

Opposite page:
Crew members working with
the crown line. Gloves are
standard equipment for both
pilots and crews.

Walla Walla Balloon Stampede
Ed Dosien

This page:
Deflation tops. Below, a pilot and
guests stand in maneuvering vent, in
light from the throat of the balloon.

Grand Teton Balloon Race
Ed Dosien

61

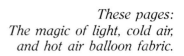

Walla Walla Balloon Stampede
Ed Dosien

*These pages:
The magic of light, cold air,
and hot air balloon fabric.*

Quechee Balloon Festival
Ed Dosien

Walla Walla Balloon Stampede
Ed Dosien

Calgary Stampede Balloon Race
Bob Brown

Albuquerque Balloon Fiesta
Ed Dosien

Albuquerque Balloon Fiesta
Ed Dosien

Albuquerque Balloon Fiesta
Ed Dosien

Canadian Fantasy Festival
Ed Dosien

These pages:
Crouched inside the uprights of gondolas, pilots hit the burners, heating the air inside envelopes as crew members hold open the throats of the balloons. As envelopes begin to lift off the ground to upright positions, other crew members hold the crown lines of the balloons to control the rising of the envelopes.

Battle Creek Balloon Championshi
Ed Dosie

Albuquerque Balloon Fiest
Bob Brow

U.S. National Balloon Championship
Ed Dosien

Opposite page:
Kodak Balloonfest
Ed Dosien

U.S. National Balloon Championship
Ed Dosien

A cold-air inflator fan is moved out of the way when hot-air inflation begins. Crew members hold open the throat of a balloon as a stream of propane flame heats the air inside the envelope.

The hundreds of separate pieces of fabric in this patchwork balloon glow like colored glass during inflation. The pilot looks straight into the interior of the balloon while aiming the burners into the throat of the envelope.

Kodak Balloonfest
Ed Dosien

Kodak Balloonfest
Ed Dosien

Opposite page and pages 70 and 71: Pilots' final burner, cable, and line adjustments before launch.

Kentucky Derby Balloon Race
Ed Dosien

Senators' Classic
Ed Dosien

Canadian Fantasy Festival
Ed Dosien

Quechee Balloon Festival
Ed Dosien

Looking up the throat of an upright envelope is like looking into a gigantic kaleidoscope.

Walla Walla Balloon Stampede
Bob Brown

Walla Walla Balloon Stampede
Ed Dosien

73

Holding down the basket of a balloon ready to become airborne. After a launch official gives the pilot permission to launch, the pilot tells the crew "Hands off," and the balloon ascends.

Walla Walla Balloon Stampede
Ed Dosien

Calgary Stampede Balloon Race
Bob Brown

Albuquerque Balloon Fiesta
Ed Dosien

Atlanta Balloon Festival
Ed Dosien

*Like some atavistic rite, people
gather to watch other people
mysteriously rise off the ground.*

Walla Walla Balloon Stampede
Ed Dosien

U.S. National Balloon Championship
Ed Dosien

...nta Balloon Festival
...Dosien

Launch

"An airplane is for getting somewhere.
A balloon is for getting away." (Pilot)

On one festival field, a bagpiper squeals and squawks his celebration of the launch, while on another, Gustav Holst's "The Planets" spreads majestically from a PA system. Like countless crowds since hot-air and gas balloons first rose in 18th century France, the crowds at the Great Balloon Festival watch in wonder, cheer, as people rise into the air, defying gravity, breaking through the ties of earth. A little boy jumps up and down, screaming with excitement.

The rising sun glows through fabric as through colored glass, then spectators shade their eyes as balloons pass the sun. Above, burners breathe like dragons, and propane flames flash inside globes of nylon. As you watch a balloon passing overhead, the sky moves.

A clipper ship design sails past clouds. A carousel balloon turns, while below it a calliope tape plays from the chase vehicle. "I'd like to ride on the white horse," a little girl says, pointing at the merry-go-round figures. Cowboys sixty feet high ride across an envelope, moving as the pilot vents, slowly turning the scene for the spectators. Roses rise. A soda pop can ascends, along with a battery, a propane tank, a smiling gas pump with flopping hose arms.

Some spectators stare open-mouthed while others smile broadly and others point, clap, snap photographs, wave.

The balloons float away like reverie. Shrinking along with the diminishing sound of burners, they become pins on the sky's blue coat, buttons, gumdrops; they seem painted in the sky, seem stuck in air, become constellations.

The chase crews drive off the field, their task just beginning. ∎ 77

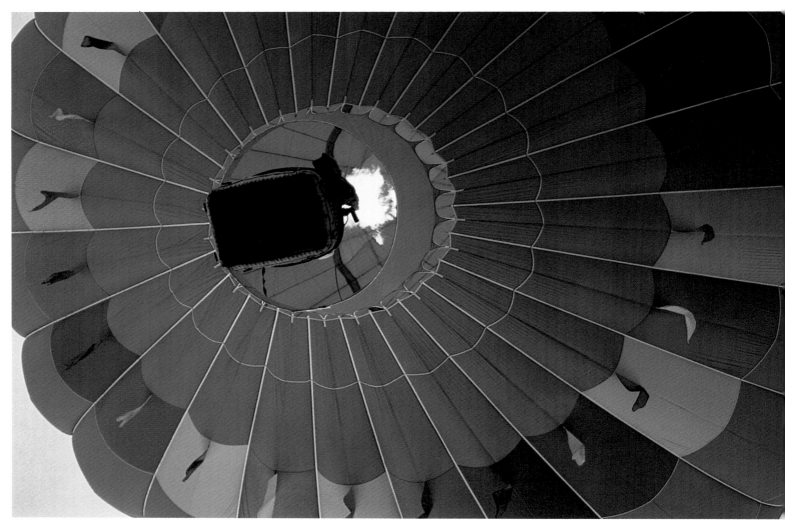

Quechee Balloon Festi
Ed Dos

Festival de Montgolfier
Joe Ni

Page 79:
Albuquerque Balloon Fiesta
Ed Dosien

The excitement, wonder, and fascination of an ascension. (For a continuation of this lift-off, see page 82.)

Kentucky Derby Balloon Race
Ed Dosien

Atlanta Balloon Festival
Ed Dosien

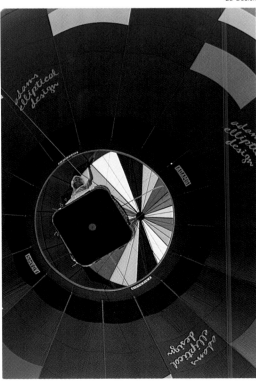

These pages:
Great Balloon Festival crowds
come in all sizes – from the
Driggs, Idaho, spectators
squinting into the rising sun on
a chill morning to the
thousands massed in the
Louisville Fairgrounds.

Kentucky Derby Balloon Rac
Ed Dosie

Kentucky Derby Balloon Rac
Ed Dosie

Previous page and this page:
As the balloon rises, the crowd
and chase vehicles shrink in
the lens of the photographer's
camera until the Louisville
horizon rises at the top of the
page.

Kentucky Derby Balloon Race
Ed Dosie

Grand Teton Balloon Race
Ed Dosien

Atlanta Balloon Festival
Ed Dosien

Snowmass Balloon Festival
Bob Brown

Conner Prairie Balloon Classic
Ed Dosien

Albuquerque Balloon Fiesta
Ed Dosien

*Opposite page:
From a leisurely, picnicking
crowd at an Indiana pioneer
settlement to Albuquerque's
Balloon Fiesta Park.*

Atlanta Balloon Festival
Ed Dosien

Snowmass Balloon Festival
Bob Brown

Albuquerque Balloon Fiesta
Ed Dosien

Walla Walla Balloon Stampede
Bob Brown

Walla Walla Balloon Stampede
Ed Dosien

Atlanta Balloon Festival
Ed Dosien

These pages:
Above Walla Walla High
School, Aspen Valley, and
Calgary's Stampede Grounds
and Olympic Saddledome

Snowmass Balloon Festival
Bob Brown

Albuquerque Balloon Fiesta
Ed Dosien

Above:
The first of three waves of 600
balloons ascending at the
Albuquerque International Hot
Air Balloon Fiesta.

Calgary Stampede Balloon Race
Bob Brown

Snowmass Balloon Festival
Bob Brown

Albuquerque Balloon Fiesta
Bob Brown

Albuquerque Balloon Fiesta
Ed Dosien

Albuquerque Balloon Fiesta
Bob Brown

Albuquerque Balloon Fiesta
Ed Dosien

Page 89:
Grand Teton Balloon Race
Ed Dosien

Canadian Fantasy Festival
Ed Dosien

Kodak Balloonfest
Ed Dosien

Snowmass Balloon Festival
Bob Brown

Opposite page:
Kodak Balloonfest
Ed Dosien

Kodak Balloonfest
Ed Dosien

Albuquerque Balloon Fiesta
Ed Dosien

Albuquerque Balloon Fiesta
Ed Dosien

Albuquerque Balloon Fiesta
Ed Dosien

Walla Walla Balloon Stampede
Ed Dosien

Snowmass Balloon Festival
Bob Brown

Calgary Stampede Balloon Race
Bob Brown

A crew member wrestles with "Dino." The cavern of the Dinosaur's open jaws is a popular spot for spectators to pose for the camera.

Fantasy Shapes

"It's Mickey, Mickey, Mickey!"
(Young spectator)

The crowds at the Great Balloon Festival converge in a single area of the festival site. A spectator wondering what is causing the mysterious shift of a mass of people looks over heads, sees a gigantic black ear growing in the air. A Mickey Mouse balloon is being inflated.

At balloon meets across North America, as other balloons drift into the distance, balloons of very special shape begin to grow out of the ground, drawing crowds, shouts, clapping. The Dinosaur, the Elephant, and the Flying Saucer, Mickey Mouse and Donald Duck, Tony the Tiger, Mr. Peanut – all inflate into the shapes of fantasy.

Noses and ears sprout. The peanut in a top hat stands upright while little green men descend a saucer stairway. The pink elephant levitates. The prehistoric monster climbs the sky.

To festival crowds, these and other whimsical balloon forms are the highlights of any given meet. Among the balloon family of "special shapes," some of these – Mickey, Donald, Tony, Mr. Peanut – are technically corporate balloons, while others – the Dinosaur, the Elephant, the Flying Saucer – are not. No matter which category each of these balloons is in, however, each evokes delight in spectators of any age.

Because special-shape balloons are built in multiple compartments, the more special the shape the more special the challenge the balloon creates for a pilot. Those balloons with appendages built off the standard balloon shape are little more difficult to handle than a standard balloon. Exceptionally horizontal or vertical shapes, though, require minimal wind for inflation and landing. ∎

Canadian Fantasy Festival
Ed Dosie

These pages:
Cartoon characters associated
with two major American
businesses: Kellogg's and Walt
Disney Productions. The animal
creations entertain crowds as
costumed figures as well as
balloons.

Battle Creek Balloon Championship
Ed Dosien

Battle Creek Balloon Championship
Ed Dosie

Battle Creek Balloon Championship
Ed Dosie

Battle Creek Balloon Championship
Ed Dosien

Battle Creek Balloon Championship
Ed Dosien

These pages:
These fabric fantasies elicit
many jokes about surprising
farmers, motorists, or inebriated
individuals.

Below:
Cat and Mouse "Hare" balloons.

Battle Creek Balloon Championship
Ed Dosien

Festival de Montgolfieres
Ed Dosien

Albuquerque Balloon Fiesta
Bob Brown

99

Canadian Fantasy Festival
Ed Dosier

 Kodak Balloonfest
Bob Brown

A corporate pilot tosses a marker towards a target in a competitive event.

Corporate Balloons

"Billboards in the sky."   (Balloonist)

Many of the balloons at the Great Balloon Festival promote a product or service through graphic designs on envelopes, special balloon shapes, or simply through advertising banners attached to the balloons.

Corporate balloons have become an increasingly popular advertising medium for small businesses and large corporations alike. For any organization wanting to disseminate its name and logo in a pleasing, soft-sell medium, hot air balloons are a fitting choice.

Balloons are traditionally associated with healthy early mornings, blue sunny skies, freedom, serenity, individuality – an appealing context for a commercial message. Also, seven-stories high or designed in unusual shapes, balloons always get attention. Colors moving in the sky are irresistible to the eye, giving hot air balloons a substantial advertising reach while in free flight along crowded freeways or tethered in high-traffic areas.

Budweiser, Chevron, Circus Circus, Coca Cola, Friexnet, J & B Rare Scotch Whisky, Kodak, Molson's, Oldsmobile, Pontiac, Red Lobster, RE/MAX, Seven-Up, Stroh's, and U.S. West are among those businesses whose brightly-designed balloons of standard shape are highly visible in balloon meets and festivals across North America.

Shaped corporate balloons such as the Chrysler star logo, the London *Financial Times* newspaper, the Pepsi soft drink can, the Shell gas pump, the Rayovac battery, and the Virgin Airlines 747 – uniquely designed as logos or products – always draw the attention of the public. Balloonists generally concur that special shapes have a special future in corporate ballooning.

For a pilot of a corporate balloon, professionalism is crucial. Because the balloon and everything associated with it is a promotional image of the company, the successful corporate pilot is careful to maintain high standards of appearance for both the van and the balloon and high standards of performance for the entire uniformed crew. ∎

Canadian Fantasy Festival
Ed Dosien

Canadian Fantasy Festival
Ed Dosien

101

Albuquerque Balloon Fiesta
Ed Dosien

Conner Prairie Balloon Classic
Ed Dosien

Canadian Fantasy Festival
Ed Dosien

Kentucky Derby Balloon Race
John Liniger

Kodak Balloonfest
Ed Dosien

While being a "special shape," the soft-drink can shape is now so standard it can be ordered by model number from a balloon manufacturer.

Kodak Balloonfest
Bob Brown

103

CORPORATE BALLOONS

These pages:
Most corporate balloons are brightly-colored standard balloon shapes emblazoned with a company logo. Modifications of the standard construction range from a clown face in high relief to a jumbo jet flying through a cloud.

Canadian Fantasy Festival
Ed Dosien

Albuquerque Balloon Fiesta
Ed Dosien

Custom-painted balloon trailers are an important part of the corporate balloon package. Some corporations have two or more balloon teams traveling in different areas simultaneously.

Battle Creek Balloon Championship
Ed Dosien

Conner Prairie Balloon Classic
Ed Dosien

Kentucky Derby Balloon Race
Ed Dosien

Kentucky Derby Balloon Race
Ed Dosien

Calgary Stampede Balloon Race
Bob Brown

Albuquerque Balloon Fiesta
Bob Brown

Kodak Balloonfest
Ed Dosien

Albuquerque Balloon Fiesta
Ed Dosien

These pages:
The Chrysler "Pentastar" and the
London Financial Times *newspaper are*
unusual shapes which draw attention
even in a crowd of balloons.

(The 20,000 characters in the text on
the newspaper balloon were painted by
hand. Combined with objective news
are personal comments of the workers
and the names of people who worked
on the project.)

Albuquerque Balloon Fiesta
Bob Brown

Filming of a Commercial

During the Great Balloon Festival, a group of corporate balloons of a single company gathers near Fenton, Michigan, for a unique balloon event: the filming of a television commercial to be aired across the United States and Canada.

The balloons participating in the filming are part of the balloon fleet of RE/MAX International, Inc., a real estate franchise company whose logo is a red, white, and blue balloon with the accompanying slogan, "Above the Crowd!®" Comprised of scores of balloons, the RE/MAX fleet is the largest corporate balloon fleet in the world.

A gyroscopic camera attached to a helicopter records most of the film footage of the launch and flight of the balloons while ground camera crews supplement the footage of the helicopter camera. At the same time, photographers – both on the ground and in balloons – record their own versions of the event.

Coordinating the launch and flight of the balloons presented unusual challenges for the filmmaker, from grouping the ascension to coding the balloons with different colored streamers for the benefit of the chase crews. For a verbal account of the filming, see "On the Air," page 202.

Opposite Page:
Ed Dosien

Bob Brown

Ed Dosien

Ed Dosien

Ed Dosien

Bob Brown

Bob Brown

Bob Brow

Ed Dosie

Pages 112-113:
Ed Dosien

Rusty Westfall

Ed Dosien

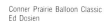
Conner Prairie Balloon Classic
Ed Dosien

This page:
A relative of the earliest hot-air and gas balloons, toy balloons are a common sight at balloon festivals.

Kodak Balloonfest
Ed Dosien

Festival Activities

"Ballooning brings out the kid in everybody." (Spectator)

As balloons drift into the distance and the sky clears, the midways of the Great Balloon Festival fill with crowds again. Lines form from food concessions enveloped in the rich smells of food, people in Ontario ordering back-bacon sandwiches, halibut and chips; in Georgia, barbecued chicken or ribs; in Iowa, fresh sweet corn, pork tenderloins; in New Mexico, breakfast burritos, green chili burgers.

The festival-goers crowd around souvenir counters, selecting festival tee-shirts, patches, and pins. They look at the creations of vendors, at ceramic balloon mobiles, balloon magnets, hanging cloth balloons with miniature teddy bears in the baskets. Multi-colored windsocks twirl in the breeze.

Clowns and people in costumes of dogs, tigers, whales, bend over and talk to children, pose for photographs, sell programs, hand out toy helium balloons. A clown sitting on a chair surrounded by children paints balloons on cheeks. Mimes carry a pane of imaginary glass through the crowd. One juggler balances a chair on a finger while another keeps balls circling in the air before fascinated eyes. Cloggers dance on a village green while well-known entertainers perform on a sound stage.

There are high school bands, skateboarders, a library booksale, a parade of antique cars, skydivers, airshows, and tents offering shade and a place to sit and watch the crowd. Many spectators bring their own chairs and umbrellas, private box seats looking out upon festival events. ■ 117

Festival-going can be exhausting on a hot day. (On a hill in the distance sits a cold air balloon, a promotional medium derived from the hot air balloon.)

Kodak Balloonfest
Ed Dosien

Albuquerque Balloon Fiesta
Bob Brown

Albuquerque Balloon Fiesta
Bob Brown

Kodak Balloonfest
Ed Dosien

Sacramento Balloon Festival
Ed Dosien

Battle Creek Balloon Championship
Ed Dosien

Battle Creek Balloon Championship
Ed Dosien

These pages:
Hand-made miniature balloons come in different forms and materials. Some concessionaires travel from one balloon meet to another, selling the merchandise they themselves created during the off-season months.

After a launch of hot air balloons, children enjoy a cold-air relative of the original balloons.

Kodak Balloonfest
Ed Dosien

Kodak Balloonfest
Ed Dosien

Free Flight

"I used to dream when I was young that I was flying, swimming through air. Later, I found that flying in a balloon is your own little vacation. No one can bother you." (Pilot)

The launch field, with thousands of faces looking up, arms waving, sinks away beneath the basket, and the ground shrinks and slides away under you, as though it is moving and you are not. The balloon moves with the wind, is virtually part of the wind itself, so you feel no sensation of movement, no air against your face, no vibration of the basket, only the suede rim of the gondola beneath your fingers. Detached from the earth, you drift along as in dream. The air around you is so clear and serene that you feel you can step out of the basket and walk across the sky.

Above festival grounds across the United States and Canada, passengers feel that sensation of balloon flight for the first time. They hear the blast of the burner and feel the heat of the flame upon their faces. They are surprised by how the world looks from up there, especially those flying over their own neighborhoods and seeing them from that height for the first time, seeing where a familiar street actually ends and another begins, where their own house is in relation to the countryside or town around it.

"When you're in a balloon," says one pilot flying in a mountain valley, layers of ridges and peaks stretching out in all directions, "you have 360 degrees of scenery below you, and on a clear morning you can see sixty miles and more. In a balloon, there's time to see things."

There is much to see for both pilots and passengers flying from festival sites across North America. While some fly over Louisville, Calgary, Phoenix, others look down upon New Mexico desert, Alberta plains, Iowa farmland, Vermont forest, Colorado mountains. Some cross lakes, rivers, descending to "splash and dash," floating on the surface of the water right along with their reflected selves. Ascending, brushing through treetops, they rise high over the countryside, sail with the clouds.

Below, traffic slows on freeways, and some drivers pull off the road to look up at balloons floating overhead. People come out of their houses, stand on front porches, in back yards, looking up.

In a balloon floating over a green field, a passenger sees a round shadow moving across the ground, realizes it is the shadow of the balloon in which she is riding. She waves, and the shadow of her arm waves back. ∎

122

FREE FLIGHT

Preceding page:
Quechee Balloon Festival
Ed Dosien

Opposite page:
Atlanta Balloon Festival
Ed Dosien

Canadian Fantasy Festival
Ed Dosien

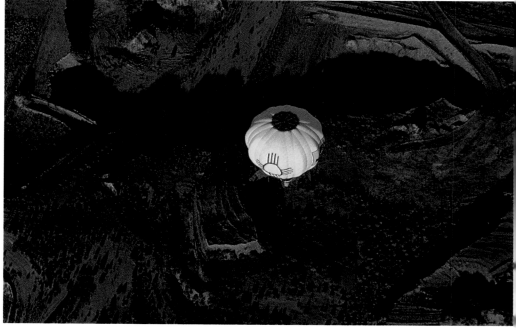

Albuquerque Balloon Fiesta
Ed Dosien

Snowmass Balloon Festival
Bob Brown

Canadian Fantasy Festival
Ed Dosien

Quechee Balloon Festival
Ed Dosien

Atlanta Balloon Festival
Ed Dosien

Grand Teton Balloon Race
Ed Dosien

FREE FLIGHT

These pages:
Sport balloons and non-competitive
"fiesta" balloons radiate with primary
colors against blue skies.

Snowmass Balloon Festival
Ron McCain

Battle Creek Balloon Championship
Ed Dosier

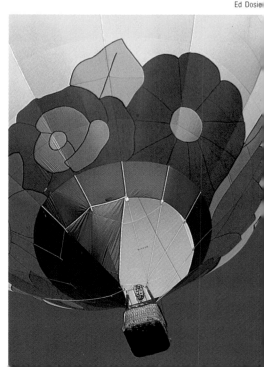

Albuquerque Balloon Fiesta
Bob Brown

Kentucky Derby Balloon Race
Bob Brown

129

FREE FLIGHT

These pages:
Pilots are constantly aware of the effects
of different kinds of terrain on the flying
of a balloon. They know that the moisture
from wooded areas and water tends to
draw a balloon lower while the thermal
activity from dry and open areas tends to
lift the balloon.

Splash and drift. Instead of splashing
down and immediately ascending, this
pilot has set his balloon down on the
water and is drifting with the river
current.

Battle Creek Balloon Championship
Ed Dosien

Canadian Fantasy Festival
Ed Dosien

U.S. National Balloon Championship
Ed Dosier

Battle Creek Balloon Championship
Ed Dosien

Above:

Balloons, like clouds, cast shadows on the land. Pilots are aware that balloon shadows can frighten livestock, but when no livestock is present, "flying the terrain" is one of the pleasures of ballooning.

Flying in mountainous areas is challenging for both fixed-wing and balloon pilots. The drainage of air down mountainsides creates "box" winds in mountain valleys, enabling a balloon to fly different directions at different altitudes, while wind currents above ridges will change a balloon's speed.

Snowmass Balloon Festival
Bob Brown

Atlanta Balloon Festival
Ed Dosien

Quechee Balloon Festival
Ed Dosien

Albuquerque Balloon Fiesta
Ed Dosien

Clockwise:
Balloons over a variety of terrains: red
Georgia clay beside an airstrip closed for
balloon competition; New Mexico desert;
a Kansas wheat field; a gravel pit; an
Arizona landscape of desert, cultivated
land, suburbs, and mountains.

Kodak Balloonfest
Ed Dosien

These pages:
Balloon baskets vary in size from a
model suitable for one to three people
to a model large enough to carry
several paying passengers.

Albuquerque Balloon Fiesta
Ed Dosien

Opposite page:
U.S. National Balloon Championship
Ed Dosien

U.S. National Balloon Championship
Ed Dosien

Albuquerque Balloon Fiesta
Ed Dosien

Snowmass Balloon Festival
Bob Brown

139

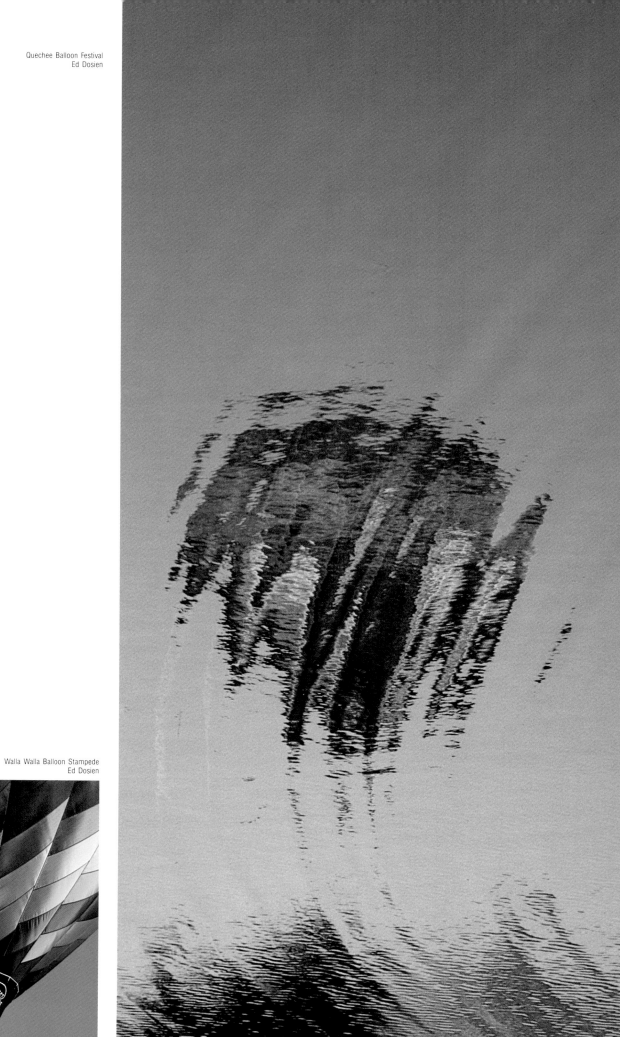

Quechee Balloon Festival
Ed Dosien

Walla Walla Balloon Stampede
Ed Dosien

Quechee Balloon Festival
Ed Dosien

Snowmass Balloon Festival
Ron McCain

Conner Prairie Balloon Classic
Ed Dosien

A balloon vehicle customized from unique balloon taillights to personalized license plate. The balloons painted on the door represent the history of hot air ballooning, from the first manned balloon of the Montgolfier brothers to the modern hot air balloon.

Walla Walla Balloon Stampede
Ed Dosien

Quechee Balloon Festival
John Liniger

Quechee Balloon Festival
John Liniger

Walla Walla Balloon Stampede
Ed Dosien

Opposite page:
A pilot performs
a Splash and Dash
while photographers
take pictures of
each other.

Quechee Balloon Festival
Ed Dosien

Walla Walla Balloon Stampede
Ed Dosien

Battle Creek Balloon Championship
Ed Dosien

*Opposite page:
A solo pilot in a
basket with a
numbered
competition
banner.*

U.S. National Balloon Championship
Ed Dosien

Kodak Balloonfest
Ed Dosien

Battle Creek Balloon Championship
Ed Dosien

Battle Creek Balloon Championship
Ed Dosien

U.S. National Balloon Championship
Ed Dosier

Walla Walla Balloon Stampede
Ed Dosien

148

Kentucky Derby Balloon Race
Ed Dosien

Calgary Stampede Balloon Race
Bob Brown

Quechee Balloon Festival
Ed Dosien

149

Snowmass Balloon Festival
Bob Brown

Senators' Classic
Ed Dosien

Atlanta Balloon Festival
Ed Dosien

Albuquerque Balloon Fiesta
Ed Dosien

151

A balloon bearing the symbol of the state of Colorado floats above the Colorado Rockies.

Snowmass Balloon Festival
Lea Ann Bailey

While balloons below drift a single direction on a lower wind, one pilot ascends a mile high to find a "box" wind which carries the balloon in the opposite direction, back towards the launch site.

Walla Walla Balloon Stampede
Ed Dosien

Snowmass Balloon Festival
Bob Brown

Quechee Balloon Festival
Ed Dosien

In Southeastern Washington
state, a balloon passes over
a stepped spawning-run
for salmon.

Walla Walla Balloon Stampede
Ed Dosien

U.S. National Balloon Championship
Ed Dosien

Kodak Balloonfest
Ed Dosien

U.S. National Balloon Championship
Ed Dosien

Festival de Montgolfieres
Ed Dosien

Festival de Montgolfieres
Ed Dosien

Battle Creek Balloon Championship
Ed Dosien

Festival de Montgolfieres
Ed Dosien

Battle Creek Balloon Championship
Ed Dosien

Albuquerque Balloon Fiesta
Ed Dosier

Battle Creek Balloon Championship
Ed Dosier

Albuquerque Balloon Fiesta
Ed Dosien

U.S. National Balloon Championship
Ed Dosien

159

Albuquerque Balloon Fiesta
Ed Dosien

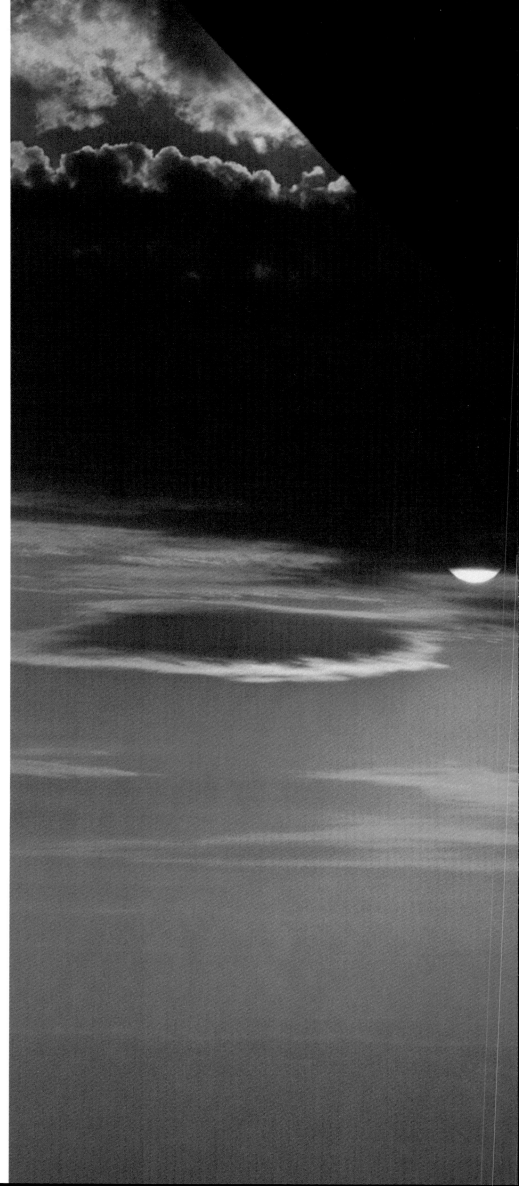

U.S. National Balloon Championship
Ed Dosien

Albuquerque Balloon Fiesta
Ed Dosien

Albuquerque Balloon Fiesta
Ed Dosien

These pages:
After competition balloonists track pilot balloons to determine off-field launch sites, they fly as close as they can to a target in order to toss a "baggie" marker, with streamer, closer than anyone else. Competition judges at the target take great care in measuring pilots' tosses.

U.S. National Balloon Championsh
Ed Dosie

Canadian Fantasy Festival
Ed Dosien

Albuquerque Balloon Fiesta
Ed Dosien

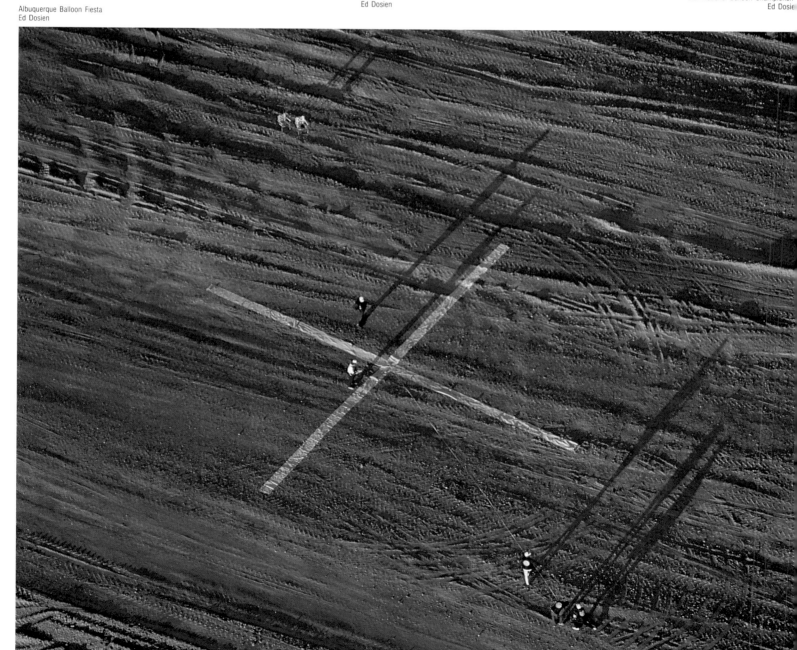

162

Bruce Comstock, World Champion, and National Champion several times over, following the flight of a pilot balloon through a range finder. Around his neck is a compass for plotting wind direction.

Competition

"It's always easier to fly a task after you've completed it." (Pilot)

Festival balloons fly off the field to complete competitive "tasks" while other balloons fly towards the field.

Festival names like "The Great Balloon Race" and the phrase "Balloon racing team," painted on chase vehicles, evoke images of balloons careening across the sky toward a finish line and an exultant pilot holding arms aloft in victory. Anyone attending a balloon meet soon learns that "balloon race" is a contradiction in terms.

Piloting skill in flying a balloon from one point to another – not speed of flight – is what wins most competitive events. Because a balloon cannot be "steered," flying skill is demonstrated by a pilot's ascending or descending to winds which will carry the balloon in the desired direction.

The most common balloon task is the **Hare and Hounds,** reminiscent of an English fox hunt. A "Hare" balloon launches from the festival site first, followed about fifteen minutes later by the "Hounds," which attempt to follow the Hare's course. The spot the Hare lands is marked with a bright cloth "X," and the Hound pilot who drops a marker closest to the center of the target wins the event.

Other competitive tasks carried out at some distance from the launch site are **Judge-Declared Goals**, in which the target is chosen by the judges and the coordinates announced before the flight, and **Pilot-Declared Goals**, individual targets pre-determined by each pilot. While enjoyable for pilots, these tasks are not usually witnessed by spectators.

Crowds, though, are treated to feats of navigational skill as balloons launched from adjacent areas float toward the site one by one. Fly-in tasks are variations of the **CNTE (Controlled Navigational Trajectory Event)**, in which pilots select a launch spot outside the field, from which they can use the winds at various altitudes to carry them over a target or prize on the launch site.

Fly-in events give spectators a chance to see which pilots are most skillful at maneuvering their balloons at different altitudes in order to approach the target. The task can be simply a toss of a marker onto an "X," or any number of other crowd-pleasing events, such as key grabs and fishing derbies.

Competitions range from serious – as at the United States, North American, Canadian, and World Championships – to simply fun. Corresponding prizes include cash, cars, cameras, and digital clocks. While most pilots agree that competition is challenging and sharpens flying skills, they also agree that competition is not for everyone. Some pilots thrive on it, while others would much prefer simply to fly. ■

163

*Above and right:
Two views of a pilot
zeroing in on an off-
site target in a Hare
and Hounds event.*

164

This page:
Pilots toss, and markers stream
towards "X" targets.

Battle Creek Balloon Championship
Ed Dosien

Battle Creek Balloon Championship
Ed Dosien

Canadian Fantasy Festival
Ed Dosien

Conner Prairie Balloon Classic
Ed Dosien

Opposite page, top:
A pilot studies an area map
prior to a crew member's
release of a pilot balloon.

Waiting spectators will not see
balloons descend close to this
target between dangerous
power lines.

Kentucky Derby Balloon Race
Ed Dosien

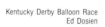

Grand Teton Balloon Race
Ed Dosien

Opposite page, bottom left:
Judges and spectators in a hay
field watch the target-approach
of a competition balloon.

The number of red streamers
on and around this purple
"X" indicates the closeness of
competition in this Kentucky
Derby Festival Great Balloon
Race. As it turned out, the top
three winners were all within
one foot and one inch of the
center of the target.

167

A pilot and his navigator – flying a judge-declared "task" – follow the assigned coordinates.

Kodak Balloonfest
Ed Dosien

Canadian Fantasy Festival
Ed Dosien

Opposite page:
Spectators watch a host of Albuquerque balloons approach the target spread out on sandy New Mexico ground.

Albuquerque Balloon Fiesta
Ed Dosien

Beside a Key Grab pole is the balloon and vehicle of the sponsor contributing a free car to any pilot lucky or skillful enough to guide a balloon in close and snatch a pair of car keys from the top of the pole.

168

Albuquerque Balloon Fiesta
Ed Dosien

Opposite page:
A pilot and a pleased "first rider" after a soft landing.

Festival de Montgolfieres
Ed Dosien

Closed down for the balloon festival, the Walla Walla airport becomes a balloon landing site.

Walla Walla Balloon Stampede
Ed Dosien

Battle Creek Balloon Championship
Ed Dosien

Festival de Montgolfieres
Ed Dosien

Landing

"Soft landings." (Balloonist saying)

After a balloon lifts off the launch area and is in flight, the ground crew piles into the chase vehicle, and the crew chief drives off the field in pursuit of the balloon. Ideally, the navigator is a local volunteer who knows the area, knows which streets go through, which bridges are out, which freeway exits lead to which country roads. An out-of-town crew is careful to acquire a local map.

Keeping the balloon in sight, the chase crew follows it during rush-hour traffic, through industrial parks, into labyrinthine subdivisions, across farmland, trying to mirror the balloon's flight. For crews in radio contact with the pilot, keeping sight of the balloon is not as crucial as it is for crews without a radio.

Once the pilot has decided upon a landing site accessible to the vehicle and begins to descend, the chase crew drives as close to the balloon as it can so as not to lose sight of it behind trees or buildings. On rare occasions, when the crew is already waiting for a descending balloon, the crew can walk the basket right up onto the back of a chase truck or trailer.

"One of the reasons I like ballooning and never get tired of it," says one pilot, "is because you never quite know where you're going to land."

During the descent, the pilot tells the

171

172

Opposite page:
A deflated envelope ready
to be repacked.

Crew hefting an envelope
bag into the back of a
chase truck.

Walla Walla Balloon Stampede
Ed Dosien

All packed up: envelope, basket,
and inflator fan.

Battle Creek Balloon Championship
Ed Dosien

passenger to stand facing the direction of landing, to hold tightly to the uprights, and to
bend the knees. The pilot also cautions the
passenger to remain in the basket after the
landing so that the balloon will not lift off
again.

The chase crew arrives with permission from
the landowner, the pilot pulls the deflation
top, the envelope sinks to the ground, and the
crew packs up, stuffing the envelope back into
its bag. After the envelope, burners and basket
are all packed into the chase vehicle, the crew
is ready for a traditional ballooning ceremony
celebrating the passenger's first balloon flight.

The pilot uncorks a bottle of champagne.
Champagne has been a ballooning tradition
since shortly after the first, unmanned flight of
a gas balloon, in 1783, when peasants attacked
the deflating envelope with pitchforks, believing
it was some sort of monster from the sky. On
later manned flights, it became common for
pilots to carry champagne to offer farmers and
landowners.

The "first rider" is then treated to the
balloonists' christening. While baptising the in-
itiate with champagne, the pilot reads the
"Balloonist's Prayer," a poem reputedly com-
posed by an Irish monk in the early days of
ballooning:

> *May the winds welcome you with*
> *softness.*
> *May the sun bless you with his*
> *warm hands.*
> *May you fly so high and so well*
> *that God joins you in laughter*
> *and sets you gently back*
> *into the loving arms*
> *of Mother Earth.*

Quechee Balloon Festival
Ed Dosien

■   173

Grand Teton Balloon Race
Ed Dosien

Festival de Montgolfieres
Ed Dosien

U.S. National Balloon Championship
Ed Dosien

Albuquerque Balloon Fiesta
Ed Dosien

A popular landing site.

LANDING

Opposite page:
In the propane line,
filling tanks for the
next flight.

Emptying propane tanks on
the desert prior to shipping
balloon home.

Grand Teton Balloon Race
Ed Dosien

Walla Walla Balloon Stampede
Ed Dosien

LANDING

Opposite page:
Quechee Balloon Festival
Ed Dosien

Packing up the envelope.

U.S. National Balloon Championship
Ed Dosien

Grand Teton Balloon Race
Ed Dosien

Another safe flight.

Grand Teton Balloon Race
Ed Dosien

Senators' Classic
Ed Dosien

In the propane line.

Grand Teton Balloon Race
Ed Dosien

Opposite page:
Packing up the burners.

Walla Walla Balloon Stampede
Bob Brown

Battle Creek Balloon Championship
Ed Dosien

After a high-wind landing, a crew prepares to carry the balloon basket out of a field to the chase vehicle.

Walla Walla Balloon Stampede
Ed Dosien

Festival de Montgolfieres
Ed Dosien

Opposite page:
Learning the ropes – the
traditional chain knot
on the envelope bag.

Walla Walla Balloon Stampede
Ed Dosien

U.S. National Balloon Championship
Ed Dosien

U.S. National Balloon Championship
Ed Dosien

U.S. National Balloon Championship
Ed Dosien

Canadian Fantasy Festival
Ed Dosien

Balloon Glow

The Great Balloon Festival ends quietly with a gathering of balloons at dusk and yet another transformation of balloon patterns to delight the eye and the imagination. On the ground, the flights of the day behind them, the balloons become globes of rhythmic light, giant *luminarias* glowing with spurts of propane flame, synchronized spectacle. ■

Battle Creek Balloon Championship
Ed Dosien

BALLOON GLOW

Albuquerque Balloon Fiesta
Bob Brown

Albuquerque Balloon Fiesta
Bob Brown

Battle Creek Balloon Championship
Ed Dosien

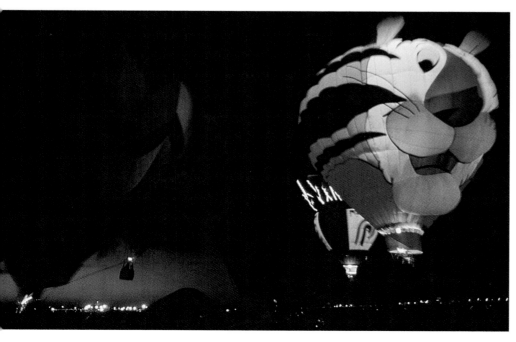

Battle Creek Balloon Championship
Ed Dosien

Post-Flight

The Individual Meets in The Great Balloon Festival

The photographs in *The Great Balloon Festival* were taken at seventeen meets across the United States and Canada throughout the 1988 ballooning season. The following sketches are a combination of information and personal observations providing a background for the photographs and giving specific attention to each festival. Readers wanting to follow a particular event through the body of the book can do so by consulting the credit lines accompanying the photographs.

189

The Senators' Classic

Scottsdale, Arizona   •   April 8-9   •   25 Balloons   •   Begun 1984

Ed Dosien

The national balloon meet season is just beginning and spring ballooning is just ending in the Arizona desert when the annual Senators' Classic is held outside Phoenix in early April. By the end of May, the desert thermals rise even before the sun, and balloons would be mired in heat, unable to lift off. In April, though, a jacket is still comfortable before dawn, when Make-A-Wish children and their parents arrive at the airfield launch area for a fun-flying day, the first of two days of ballooning.

In 1984, the Pointe Resorts created the Senators' Classic for the Make-A-Wish Foundation, an international charity which raises money to grant wishes of children with life-threatening diseases. The annual fund-raising balloon rally is one of the few events of the year which brings Make-A-Wish staff members, children, and families together from throughout the Arizona chapter.

At the pilot briefing, the Balloonmeister cautions pilots that it is cotton planting time, that farmers are sensitive about balloons landing in their fields, and he urges chase crews to remain on established roads as much as possible so as not to disturb the desert environment. He points out that the Gila River Indian Reservation to the southwest is a "PZ," a prohibited zone.

As burners blast and balloon after balloon rises upright on the airstrip, children are lifted or helped into gondolas. The knuckles of a girl "first rider" whiten as she grips the rim of a rising gondola, while the girl beside her grins with excitement and waves to her family receding below.

An hour later, chase vehicles return with excited kids. The adventurers pose for photographs with Arizona Senator John McCain and costumed figures, DJ the Clown, Officer McGruff, and Debonair Hare, and they answer questions about how the ride was. One girl compresses the rare experience into three little words: "It was fun." A boy says the sky was filled with the barking of dogs and that when they were passing low over a field, he saw jack rabbits running, their ears flattened back.

Pilots enjoy participating in the Senators' Classic because "It's for a good cause," and they relish giving the kids free balloon rides. The cowboy cookout of T-bone steaks, corn on the cob, and beans, outside a restaurant overlooking the lights of Phoenix, isn't half bad either, they say. Not so relished, though, is landing in desert after the next morning's Hare and Hounds race and taking care not to rip deflated envelopes on cactus and brush.

That night, at the black-tie fund-raising dinner, one pilot tells others at a table about his gondola colliding with a clump of mesquite at the second target, and the incident leads into a cactus story about when he was a rookie pilot coming in for his first desert landing. He was heading straight towards a tall saguaro cactus, knowing he was going to hit it, thinking the top would snap right off. "It was like hitting a steel column," he says. And that story runs into talk about landing in haystacks, that haystacks are less like down pillows than they are like concrete abutments.

Sacramento Balloon Festival

Rocklin, California • April 23-24 • 70 Balloons • Begun 1988

Ed Dosien

The program cover of the first annual Sacramento Hot Air Balloon Festival is a painting of a cowboy sitting on a rock in a sunlit pasture, watching a flotilla of hot air balloons drifting over California hills. A ten-year weather study indicated this weekend as the most suitable of the year for a balloon meet, but following a stretch of warm spring weather, days of rain have turned the designated launch site to mud. Pilots and crews arriving at the warehouse headquarters on this cold and rainy Friday afternoon are undaunted. The building parking lot is filled with gaily painted balloon vehicles, many with vanity plates declaring the ballooning passion of their owners; inside, balloonists wearing jackets with balloon patches, some in caps covered with balloon pins, joke about the weather. Beyond the registration area, tables with toy helium balloon centerpieces are set for the opening night pilot party.

The next morning, balloonists driving to the new launch site in the dark peer out through rainy windshields glaring red with taillights. After weeks of media publicity, area residents hungry for color and excitement are already crowding the freeway on their way to Sacramento's first balloon fiesta. Even though weather can change drastically within a few hours, the balloonists doubt that the spectators will see the color-filled sky they had expected to see when they crawled out of bed at an ungodly hour this Saturday morning.

Parked cars line the highway near the substitute launch site, and dressed for the morning cold, carrying blankets and cameras, the crowd streams down through a soggy field to the paved area around a cluster of storage buildings. Music piping through a PA system makes even the chill morning festive. Above concessions and craft booths open for business, colored banners snap in the wind. Even though it is still before dawn, a boy huddled up in a blanket munches on a big juicy hamburger while looking at hand-painted ceramic balloons swinging from a booth canopy. A loose helium balloon blows away at an angle, rocking as it goes, and disappears into the gray morning light. After a tattered sunrise, the Balloonmeister holds a pilot briefing inside the warehouse headquarters. "It's a fireshow up there," he says. "Far too dangerous to fly." He invites the pilots to inflate their balloons for the crowd and ends with

"Think sun for tomorrow."

To a disappointed crowd, even an inflation is considerably better than nothing. As envelopes flow out of canvas bags onto a roadway, walls of people form on either side of them. "Wow, it's really getting big," a kid says, watching color stream out onto pavement. He jumps as the inflator fan roars, and as the long strip of fabric begins to ripple with air and expand, the boy bounces up and down, yelling with excitement. The giant grows out of the pavement and spreads right up to his feet. The boy leans away, cautiously reaches out a hand. Touching the living thing, he leaps back, laughing with delight. The entire crowd jerks as the pilot blasts the burner. The envelope billows, bulges. The spectators shout as the envelope rises off the concrete, and they hoot and applaud as the balloon stands upright. With his crew sitting on the gondola to keep the balloon from becoming airborne, the pilot motions the spectators to come closer. They crowd in, and as they gaze up through the throat into the colored dome of air, he explains to them how a hot air balloon works. A young woman looking up with wonder, turns, motions her male companion over. "Honey, you've got to see this."

Weather is no issue at that evening's Great Chicken Cookoff. Pilots and crews arrive in costumes from biker gangs to surfers, give it their high-spirited all in sixteen-legged races, and more than do justice to barbecued chicken dinners.

Sunday morning, the sun breaks through the clouds, but the colored banners are again streaming from their poles. The Balloonmeister gives the pilots the go-ahead to inflate and the permission to fly for any who wish to do so. The wind twists the inflating envelopes into freeform shapes. Crews strain against tether lines, wrestling with the envelopes as though with sails. The smoke of fabric scorched from long blasts of burners blows across the launch site. Standing on the rim of his gondola, a pilot in a cowboy hat bulldogs his envelope upright with a long long burn. The basket begins to drag, then swing under the rising envelope. As the pilot leaps inside, the balloon takes off like a shot. A few other balloons follow, sailing low to the ground.

191

Kentucky Derby Balloon Race

Louisville, Kentucky   •   April 30   •   50 Balloons   •   Begun 1973

An airy wire sculpture of winged Pegasus floats high in the Louisville air terminal, greeting visitors to the Kentucky Derby Festival. The week that ends with one of the world's most famous horse races begins with a Hare and Hounds "race" in which balloonists drop baggies of Kentucky bluegrass onto an "X" target. The Festival's Pegasus logo symbolically embraces both events: the flight of balloons and the horses in the Derby.

Hotel signs welcome the balloonists, and at a busy front desk, clerks adorned with balloon pins of pilots and crews already checked in, exude a Southern Hospitality so warm and friendly that a registering balloonist can't resist reaching into a pocket for a balloon pin.

The wind of Friday afternoon blows through, leaving a still, clear, pre-dawn sky on Saturday. In the parking lot behind the headquarters hotel, the balloonists meet in the early morning darkness to drive their vans and trailers in designated order to their designated positions on the launch area at the fairgrounds across the street. A local television crew interviews a balloonist wearing a rubber rabbit nose and whiskers. The pilot and his matching crew then pose for photographs beside their Hare balloon vehicle, which bears the sign, "Hare we are." Their balloon holds the Hare honor by virtue of having won the previous year's Kentucky Derby Festival Great Balloon Race. Uniformed crews, in competition for the "Best Dressed Crew" award, wave from their baskets as the procession moves out into the dark, following a route which bypasses the traffic jam through the fairgrounds' main gate.

The grass launch site is roped off until all envelopes are laid out in position. Used throughout the sixteen years of the Louisville balloon race, the site is divided into fifty areas for Hound balloons, with an additional position for the Hare balloon. At a single shot from the traditional starting cannon, the downwind Hare will begin its inflation. When the Hare is inflated, ready to lift off, the second cannon shot will signal the beginning of inflation for the Hounds. At the appointed time, the launch officers will direct the lift-off of each balloon in order, working from the south end of the fairgrounds field to the north end. The race is scheduled to begin with the 7 a.m. lift-off of the Hare balloon.

As spectators crowd against the ropes around the field, the balloonists drive onto the launch site, park in their assigned spaces, and begin laying out. A burner blasts, shooting a twenty-foot column of flame up into the darkness. After envelopes are spread out onto the grass, an announcer speaks over the PA system: "Good morning, ladies and gentlemen. Welcome to the Ken-

tucky Derby Great Balloon Race. Let the crowd in." The cannon fires the Hare balloon begins cold-air inflation, and the ropes are dropped. From the inflation area, the sound of 50,000 people rises as the crowd converges on the field. A car horn begins honking rhythmically. The Hare balloon curves with air, and as the burners blast, it rises upright to the shouts of the crowd. "What happens if the hare balloon doesn't get up?" a spectator asks. The cannon fires a second time, smoke billowing from its barrel, and at 7:03 the Hare balloon lifts off to the cheering of the crowd. Inflation fans roar, and envelopes begin growing out of the grass. Mr. Peanut, wearing a top hat and carrying a cane, stretches himself to his full length, stands, the Kentucky Fried Chicken popping up behind him, kids screaming and pointing, adults clapping. At 7:12, the sun is just breaking the horizon, lighting the flames of the Stroh's envelope, "America's only Fire-Brewed Balloon." Thousands of colored toy balloons are released as the Hound balloons begin lifting off. The crowd roars as the gentleman peanut and the setting hen rise into the sky. "Is the chicken going to win?" a little girl asks her mother. The sky is full of balloons. It is 7:15. At 7:32, the balloons are all receding into the distance, and the crowd begins leaving the launch site.

How synchronized the entire event was is revealed at the balloonists' award breakfast when it is announced that the marker of the third-place winner of the Kentucky Derby Hare and Hounds Race landed one foot, one inch from the center of the target, only one inch farther than that of the second place winner, and seven inches farther than that of the first-place winner — the closest "race" in the event's history.

After the festivities of the morning, and after a ballooner nap, several crews gather out in the Kentucky countryside for a leisurely afternoon flight. The selected launch area, used with permission, is a private airfield, and as the balloons inflate, the older couple who own the field come out to watch and are joined by a woman and her young son from the farmhouse just beyond the field, at the edge of a woods. The balloonists talk to them and, in the absence of the traditional champagne gift to landowners, give them all balloon pins. The older woman says she likes balloons, and she recalls that when her ninety-year-old stepfather was visiting them years before, nine balloons landed right in this pasture. The four balloons lift off gently in the quiet air and drift in the direction of the farmhouse. After the spectators return to their homes, a crew lies down in the fragrant spring grass, now burnished with sunset, and looks at the balloons hanging suspended above the farmhouse and the hill as though they're painted there.

Ed Dosien

Walla Walla Balloon Stampede

Walla Walla, Washington • May 12-14 • 40 Balloons • Begun 1974

At Walla Walla's champagne reception for balloonists, the town community center is crowded with townspeople, Chamber of Commerce staff, balloon crews. People throughout the hall are drinking from commemorative champagne glasses imprinted with the full-colored logo of the festival. From the rafters hang colored paper clouds and balloons prepared by a second-grade class from photographs of balloons from past stampedes. Tables are piled high with trays and bowls of relishes, salads, cheeses, drumsticks, Swedish meatballs, barbecued beef, a variety of breads. After greetings, announcements, and acknowledgements, the crowd joins in singing "Happy Birthday" to Suzie, who is twenty-one today.

The community is celebrating an event which began as a fun-flying afternoon for three balloonists back in 1974 and became a gathering of seven balloons the next year, the only year the meet has been weathered out in its fourteen-year history. For several years, a local radio station sponsored the event as a sales promotion until it grew beyond the station's resources to handle it. After the station approached the Chamber of Commerce, the Chamber manager, Nance Reznicek, took a balloon ride, listening throughout the flight to pilot Chauncey Dunn tell of the joys of ballooning. The Chamber became involved, took over full sponsorship of the festival in 1984, and now,

Ed Dosien

for the first time, is combining the stampede with two other local festivals, creating a gigantic community celebration of spring in the Walla Walla Valley. Store windows are painted with balloons, motel signs welcome ballooners, and a carnival has set up on the main street of town.

"We work hard to keep the pilots happy, the sponsors happy, and the spectators happy," Reznicek says, explaining the role of a festival manager. "In a community of this size, you have to work at all three. And I do mean 'work.' You can't just say you're going to put on a festival and expect the people to come. For one thing, items on order for it six months ago got lost somewhere on their way to Walla Walla. That's just one of the organizational nightmares you go through with an event like this. I have a staff of four that works hard on this project all year, and when the event goes off smoothly, it's because of them and all the volunteers, like all of my folks here on a Friday night. The reason you see so much excitement here is that all of these people are involved."

The down-home spirit becomes a crowd of thousands at the Wa-Hi (Walla Walla High School) launch site the next morning. Even before sunup, craft booths are open for business. Windsocks and kites, calico balloons and suncatchers are barely moving in the quiet air. From a grandstand at the edge of the field, a local radio announcer donates his talents to explaining the ballooning process and keeping the crowd informed of developments. A released helium balloon wobbles upward, then angles north. After a 5:30 sunrise over moody foothills, the announcer tells the crowd the good news from the pilot briefing: "There is a 'go.' The balloons will go up."

The balloons launch one after another into the gray sky, the announcer identifying the sponsor and pilot of each balloon, speaking jovially to the waving pilots as they pass overhead.

"We have a survival kit," says one pilot to his passengers and his crew when he is given permission to launch. "We have sugar, we have jerky, we have a tent. We're going to the wilderness." He burns, and the balloon lifts off. Just past the high school grounds, he whistles down to a horse in a pasture, calls out, "It's ok, boy, it's ok." He waves down to a woman standing in a

bathrobe at the back door of her house, looking up at the passing balloon. "Morning," he says, and toots a horn. "I smell bacon. Sorry we can't stop for breakfast. Thanks for having us come over." The woman waves. More greetings to backyard gawkers as the balloon follows the route of the Hare balloon, heading off to the northeast, most of the other balloons moving east.

Soon, "There's the target," the pilot says, looking down at an orange cloth "X" in the outfield of a community baseball diamond, the target area surrounded by scoring judges. "Here it is. Look at this. Hold onto the side rail because the basket's going to jerk a little when I throw." The bright target glides below. "Coming down. Heads up." The baggie streamer arcs out and down, and the pilot shouts down to the judges, "Second base. Second base marker." He tells his passengers his baggie is closer than anyone else's. The ground slides away below, faster now as the wind picks up. The pilot says when he first started flying balloons ten years before, he flew in this area. "I learned the hard way about landing in foothills. You never land on the downwind side in a balloon. You'll go right to the bottom, no matter what, and you start building up so much speed, it'll drag you halfway up the next one. We're going to be landing right out there in the field. There are going to be some rough landings out here this morning. Look at that balloon right over there. He's really smoking down."

He tells his passengers to face the direction the balloon is moving, hold on to the uprights, and flex the knees. He begins whistling "Stars and Stripes Forever." The ground is streaming underneath. "OK, face forward," he says. "We're cooking. We're going to hit. We're going to drag a little bit. We're going to stick a corner in. Ready? Here we go. Brace yourselves, bent knees." Burn, hit. "Swing, top's out. Here it is, here it is, here it is." Jostling drag, and the basket tips over, pilot and passenger onto another passenger with his face in a fragrant pea field.

Back at the high school festival site, one old man looks at his watch, looks at the sky, says to his friend, "Well, it's about time they'll be flying back here." Instead, a plane appears and specks of spiralling skydivers grow into bright red, white, and blue chutes, sweeping down out of the sky.

Through the day, during the antique car show, the band concerts, the volleyball tournament, the sky clears. For the spectators, the afternoon flight – to the south, past farmhouses and lush pastures – is less a flight than it is a quiet, sunny tableau. For one passenger, though, the flight is a thrilling mile-high ascent, with the pilot finding a high wind which carries the balloon back above the festival area. A venting, spiralling descent lands the balloon back near where it launched, a hundred yards or so from a community chicken barbecue, just in time for dinner.

That evening, the balloons inflate in the dark for a Balloon Glow. Illuminating a group of balloons at night by means of propane burners was the innovation of Albuquerque balloonists, who saw the similarity between glowing balloons and luminarias, candles in paper bags, which are traditionally lighted on Christmas Eve in the Southwestern United States. The Balloon Glow became part of the Albuquerque Fiesta in 1987, and the spectacular balloon display has become a popular event at balloon festivals across North America.

With the Walla Walla announcer doing the countdowns, the balloons all burn and light simultaneously, igniting the field with globes of muted color, drawing "Oooohs" and "Aaaahs" from the crowd.

193

Conner Prairie Balloon Classic

Indianapolis, Indiana • May 28 • 30 Balloons • Begun in 1980

The afternoon before millions of television viewers hear, "Gentlemen, start your engines," and the unremitting roar of the world-renowned Indianapolis 500 fills a Memorial Day holiday morning, a small and quiet hot air balloon race is held outside the city at Conner Prairie Pioneer Settlement.

Meet founder Jim Ryan explains that the Conner Prairie May Balloon Classic is not an official part of the Indy 500 festivities. The balloon race that was once sponsored by the "500" committee was launched off the track, late in the day, when there was much thermal activity from the asphalt surface, creating precarious wind conditions. A balloon mishap led to litigation and cancellation of the "500" balloon event.

Ryan started what has become the Conner Prairie May Hot Air Balloon Classic in 1980, selecting Saturday afternoon of Indy weekend for the event because the crowd in town for the race has few activity options at that time. After holding his meet at industrial parks for several years, Ryan was able to acquire the Conner Prairie site for the "race." In 1836, a group of homesteaders at Conner Prairie planned the nearby White River settlement, which grew into Indianapolis. On the site, Ryan points out a natural amphitheater of open fields surrounded by trees, at the base of a hill, which he considers a perfect launch area.

The heavily agricultural area offers few landing problems, except for a farm of thoroughbred racehorses and an animal park of camels, zebras, and llamas. Although early May is a volatile time of year for Indianapolis weather, the meet has been rained out only twice. This year, it is so dry throughout the Midwest that a farmer pilot who would normally be busy with planting is participating in the meet. The air is filled with the chirping of birds and the smell of new-mown hay. A possum lumbers out of the trees at the edge of the field, circles back to privacy. Now, near sunset, the wind has died. Ryan predicts similar weather conditions for the next day's launch.

Saturday afternoon, both the knoll above the launch field and an adjoining hill below restored pioneer cabins are covered with people at picnic tables, on blankets, sitting on lawn chairs, talking, eating fast-food fried chicken, drinking soft drinks, while kids run around and roll down the grassy slopes.

At the pilot briefing on a trailer down on the launch field, Balloonmeister Ryan's weather report and instructions are at the same time heard by the crowd through speakers up on the hill, the sound of the small actual voice on the trailer echoed an instant later by the booming voice from the loudspeaker. The inflation and launch are accompanied by an explanation of the competitive task, the name of each pilot and balloon, and a plug for each commercial balloon. The Balloonmeister notes that there are nearly the same number of balloons in the Conner Prairie Balloon Classic as there are race cars entered in the Indy 500 the next day. As the balloons lift off, helium balloons inflated by the major sponsor, *The Nobleville Daily Ledger*, are released, drifting past their *montgolfiere* relatives. The hot air balloons arc over the crowd to shouts, clapping, and picture-taking. After they have floated out of sight, soft jazz spreads over the hill from the PA, and many of the spectators remain, talking, quietly enjoying themselves as the sun sets.

Ed Dosien

Quechee Balloon Festival

Quechee, Vermont　　•　　June 17-19　　•　　15 Balloons　　•　　Begun 1980

Deep in the wooded hills of eastern Vermont, the village of Quechee celebrates the arrival of summer with a balloon festival and crafts fair. Organized by the local Chamber of Commerce, the event attracts thousands of spectators to what any visitor is likely to regard as the embodiment of a stereotypical New England village, self-contained and self-reliant, steeped in tradition. The route to the launch site is off a main highway, across a covered wooden bridge, down a main street lined with frame and brick buildings of colonial architecture, and onto the village green.

A morning flight follows the general direction of the Ottauquechee River, an Abenaki Indian name meaning "quick whirling motion." The river winds past the town, across flats, and drops through dark, primeval Quechee Gorge 165 feet below one of the highest highway bridges in the East. Chase vehicles are slowed to a stop on the bridge packed with amateur photographers clicking away at balloons floating their way.

For years, said one balloonist, area pilots have watched for an opportunity to maneuver their balloons under the bridge. This morning, a pilot drifting above the gorge in the softly moving air, sees his chance, descends. With tree limbs brushing the fabric on either side, and no additional clearance for the eighty-foot-high balloon, the pilot threads his craft into the needle's eye of bridge and chasm. Spectators on one side of the bridge lean over the railing, watching the crown of the balloon slide beneath them, while spectators on the other side watch the brightly-colored behemoth appear, grow, and the crown pass beneath the steel. To the exultant cries of the crowd, the balloon emerges unscathed, the first in popular memory to achieve the feat.

Back on the green throughout the hot day, there are fly-fishing demonstrations, chainsaw artistry, performances by cloggers and folk musicians, craft booths, a library book sale, a bingo tent. Many festival-goers choose to just sit in lawn chairs in the shade. Tickets are drawn for free balloon rides for the afternoon flight.

Late that afternoon, spectators with cameras crowd the covered wooden bridge over the Ottauquechee River, looking into the afternoon sun. Below, beneath the dam, boys in swimming trunks climb over slabs of rock, lower themselves into rushing water, and swim into the grotto under the historic Quechee mill. Above the placid water behind the dam, diners on the mill's awninged terrace look to the west for the first balloons rising from the village green over the hill. The crowd on the bridge shifts for position as a bright sport balloon rises out of the grass, arcs over to the river, the balloon's reflection spreading in the water, and descends to the surface in a "splash and dash" maneuver. Paying passengers wave to the onlookers from the gondola drifting with the current. The balloon rises, water streaming from the basket, and passes over trees lining the far bank. Passengers pluck leaves from the treetops. One by one, other balloons lift from the launch field, and chevrons and stripes of primary color curve through blue sky to the river. The balloons settle down like ducks upon the water, float with their dark, mirrored selves, and lift again. In a shifting gentle breeze, the last balloons float past the mill and over the covered bridge.

Ed Dosien

Kodak Balloonfest

Chicago / Kansas City / St. Louis   •   June 23-July 4   •   100 Balloons   •   Begun 1988

Ed Dosien

Bob Brown

The promotional concept could not be better: Celebrate the 100th anniversary of the snapshot with a ten-day, three-city extravaganza featuring hot air balloons, one of the most photogenic subjects imaginable. After fifteen months of planning, the Eastman Kodak Company is offering the public across the Midwest entertainment on a grand scale. In the elaborate festival area will be: daily morning and afternoon flights of one hundred balloons; top-name entertainers on the gigantic sound stage; a new musical play for children, "The Marvelous Balloon Time Machine," performed on its own specially-created stage; a BMX bicycle and skateboard exhibition; unique kites; corporate displays; food and souvenir concessions; clowns, jugglers; free helium balloons for all the kids. For the balloonists, the tour provides a possible 2,000 individual balloon flights in forty flight hours, and a $25,000 cash first prize out of a total prize purse of more than $60,000. Full-color programs and brochures and a full-scale promotional campaign in the three selected Midwestern cities complete the preparations for the festival.

At the Lisle, Illinois, site the afternoon before the opening day, banners are streaming in the wind as crews erect the stages and the food and exhibit tents. The flags are still streaming with wind the next morning, when the first, fly-by balloon event is cancelled. Later that day, music from the sound stage sets the festival atmosphere for a sparse crowd. Skateboarders swoop down curved wooden ramps, and a life-sized kite figure of mythical Icarus soars above the crowd, wings and legs swimming in air. In "The Marvellous Balloon Time Machine," Captain Air sings to the young crowd that he's a "Dream Pilot," and children from the audience fly in a dance with the entire costumed cast. Along the roped-off launch field, miniature fabric *montgolfieres* filled with helium balloons swing in the hot breeze.

At launch time, veteran Balloonmeister Tom Sheppard assesses weather conditions as marginal, but still flyable, and the one hundred balloons inflate to a stirring fanfare from the sound stage. Tie-off lines are loosed, and the balloons lift off in waves. The competitive task is a two-part judge-declared goal which takes the balloons over Chicago suburbs and down to brisk landings, "augering in" and "wicker knees." After one landing, as passengers excitedly discuss the flight, the pilot pops the cork from a champagne bottle into the basket at ten paces, and when they lift their plastic glasses, he jokingly toasts, "Soft landings."

That is the first and last launch out of eight flights scheduled for the Chicago leg of the tour. In briefing after briefing, the Balloonmeister is forced to deliver discouraging pilot-balloon readings. He points out that a disappointed public simply does not understand that winds can be at different velocities at different altitudes. After one weathered-out morning, a crew member in the

hotel parking lot looks out over the covered baskets, shakes his head, and says, "Sleeping giants."

Through long, windy afternoons "on hold," some of the balloonists engage in a three-man slingshot war, pleasing the crowd by shooting water balloons a couple of hundred feet at each other, occasionally scoring a hit in an opponent's basket. U.S. and Canadian crews sweat it out in a tug-of-war. Some balloonists parked near the crowd blast the burners and explain how balloons work. Afternoons when the weather permits, some pilots inflate their balloons for the crowd, especially those with special-shape balloons. A pink-and-white elephant balloon and the 130-foot dinosaur, with its great open mouth and white fabric teeth, offer the spectators glimpses of what they came to see. In the partially filled festival parking lot, a decal on a car window pictures a wind god blowing clouds over the word "Chicago." The next morning, when the pilots and crews head for Kansas City, the sky is clear and bright, and the air is still.

An opening morning fly-by from the countryside slows rush-hour traffic near Kansas City, drivers watching a sky filled with moving color, but after that, the negative "pibal" readings continue. One afternoon, under a Midwestern sky piled along the edges with hazy clouds, the few spectators on the festival site huddle in whatever shadow they can find to escape the sweltering prairie heat. The highlight of the afternoon is an inflated flying saucer balloon, just delivered from England. Spacemen walk down a step appendage, and inside the envelope, just above the throat, a little green man grins down at the gawker. At the balloonists' hotel that evening, a small, remote-controlled balloon floats around under the atrium roof, does a splash and dash in the hotel pool, much to the surprise of a swimmer. The final morning at Kansas City, a long-awaited thunderstorm arrives, bringing relief to drought-threatened farmers.

In St. Louis, the Kodak Tour joins the eighth annual V.P. Fair, a four-day super-festival featuring the largest parade in the Midwest, a Mississippi River regatta, name entertainers, and an air show opening with a parachutist drifting through the Gateway Arch. Beginning with blessedly cool weather and ending with scorching heat and a colossal fireworks display, "America's Biggest Birthday Party" draws more than two-and-a-half million people down to the river front. As for the Balloonfest, winds blowing toward Lambert Airfield force a launch-site change, and a second change the last day of the celebration.

Although turbulent weather cancelled most of the Balloonfest's scheduled launches, the pilots with the highest number of competition points at the end of the event still take home the prize money.

Grand Teton Balloon Race

Driggs, Idaho   •   July 2-4   •   35 Balloons   •   Begun 1982

Ed Dosien

In the valley on the western slope of the Grand Tetons is Pierre's Hole, the site of the Great Rocky Mountain Fair of 1832, a rip-roaring Rendezvous of mountain men, fur trading companies, and Indians. That spirited gathering ended with an attack by Gros Ventre Indians and a victory by the trappers and their Indian friends.

Now, as then, at this time of year, spring snows have melted, and silver lupine, mule-eared daisies, Indian paintbrush, and columbine are all abloom in the Tetons. They are splashes of color along the mountain road from the balloonists' headquarters down to Pierre's Hole Restaurant, in Driggs, where pilots and crew gather to whoop it up at a sponsors' reception. On the way back up the mountain that night and down to the valley in the dark the next morning, balloonists catch a lot of critters in their headlights: a moose calf, deer, a porcupine the size of a medicine ball, grouse, a coyote.

A three-quarter moon is still shining brightly at 5 a.m. as spectators in coats and blankets begin straggling from the balloon rally parking lot towards the fairgrounds building at the launch area, ready for breakfast. To the east, the sky is pale over the jagged Teton peaks. Down the misty valley and across, the mountains are shadowy forms. The morning cold makes the block of light in the open doorway all the more inviting. Inside, it's bright, warm with morning talk and the smells of the Teton Valley Cowbells' Sunrise Breakfast. Past the cashier table, cowboys in aprons are pouring batter onto sputtering griddles, flipping pancakes. Customers move down the food line, being served as they go with mounds of hash browns, scrambled eggs, ham, the flapjack cooks covering it all with a couple of inch-thick pancakes. The kitchen is crowded with women frying mountains of potatoes and eggs. A cowboy carries a kettle from the kitchen, pours it steaming into the coffee urn, stands bowlegged by the kitchen door with his thumbs hooked into the pockets of his rolled-up jeans, watching over things. When asked what the Cowbells do besides cook balloon meet breakfasts, he says, grinning, "They're like a two-hundred pound tiger. They do whatever they want."

At sunrise, spectators are hanging out around the field and fill the bleachers beside the launch area, watching the balloon crews unload the vans. An announcer on the bed of a truck welcomes the crowd, tells them the basics of what makes a hot air balloon fly, what it feels like to ride in a balloon. He bends down to hear what someone has to say to him. "Ladies and gentlemen," he says, "there are a couple of free dogs on the field. I guess that means they're free to anybody who wants them. Anyway, the balloonists would like them not to be there, because they might rip an envelope, so if they're yours, would you please go get them." He is handed new information: During today's flight there will be a wedding in one of the balloons, the Mayor

of Mountain Home, Idaho, tying the knot of the lucky couple. The Balloonmeister in white bib overalls, rainbow-striped shirt with cap to match, talks to the announcer. It's a go.

As the balloons inflate and launch against the Grand Teton backdrop, the announcer explains to the crowd that a balloon race is not actually a race, and even though the name of their balloon event says it's a race, the winds are so calm this morning that it will be just a free-flying morning. And it is, with the thirty-five balloons ascending and descending to find air currents which for an hour simply carry them around overhead or within clear sight of the launch field, giving the spectators an unusually long visual treat.

A quiet morning also gives the pilots opportunity to land and change passengers at least once, lifting them over the wide valley. Passengers look down on clumps of grazing cattle, on a network of paths between the mounds of a prairie dog village. The flights are slow, silent between burns, dreamlike. When one pilot lands in an empty pasture, his crew goes to get permission from the rancher to drive out and retrieve the balloon. Permission is given, with the condition that the balloonist take the ranch children up for a ride. Permission is accepted. Pleased children soon emerge from the wicker gondola with an adventure of the morning inside them and with balloon pins on their collars.

There are even more first riders the second morning of the rally. Back at the launch site after the flight, they are introduced to the balloonist ritual of christening. While they kneel in a row on blankets, hands behind backs, a pilot pours champagne into cups sitting in front of them and solemnly intones the "Balloonist's Prayer." The initiates bend down, grasp the cups in their teeth, and try to drink without spilling any of the precious liquid, while pilot and crew douse them with champagne. In one elaborate ceremony, a pilot kneels facing them, priest-like, lengthily recounting the early history of ballooning, and then reciting the prayer portion of the ritual. After it is over, he presents them with certificates attesting to their flight – and they pour champagne on him. If the old mountain men were to reappear in this bright summer sun of the Teton Valley, they would surely realize they were at a new kind of Rendezvous.

Thunder, lightning, and rain the morning of the Fourth of July is welcomed by the ranchers and is not resented by the balloonists, who have two days of fun-flying behind them. The Cowbells do a booming business with their Sunrise Breakfast. At an informal awards presentation at one end of the fairgrounds building, the "Big Fun" trophy, with a golden hog on top, is presented to the balloonist who was judged to have had the most fun of anybody the last few days.

197

Battle Creek Balloon Championship

Battle Creek, Michigan   •   July 9-16   •   150 Balloons   •   Begun 1981

Ed Dosien

Across the street from the balloon headquarters hotel in downtown Battle Creek, the Tony the Tiger balloon is painted on a boarded-up window of a brick building, and on the glass doors of the hotel entrance are Tony balloon stickers. The shaped face of the cartoon character associated with Kellogg's cereals is the well-known corporate balloon of a company whose name is intertwined with the name of the city in which it is located. As a major industry in the Cereal Capital, Kellogg's is the major sponsor of a balloon event which generates an estimated $25 million to $30 million in the local economy each year.

Battle Creek became involved with ballooning in a big way when it hosted the fifth World Hot Air Balloon Championship in 1981, drawing pilots from twenty-three countries, two hundred balloons, and a million spectators. The success of that event prompted the city to host the North American Championship in 1983, the Seventh World Championship in 1985, and to bid to hold the U.S. National Balloon Championship after that event left its Indianola, Iowa, site. Unsuccessful in that bid, Battle Creek's commitment to ballooning took shape as its own annual International Balloon Championship, first held in 1987.

The intense heat and dryness plaguing the entire Midwest this summer do not spare Battle Creek. After the opening ceremonies of the eight-day event, members of the honor guard of the Battle Creek Police Department are treated for heat exhaustion. But a dripping ninety-six degrees does not deter the crowd. Only a few hundred people gather for the first airshow, but by late afternoon, the crowd at Kellogg Field numbers about a quarter of a million. The heat and wind force Balloonmeister Tom Sheppard to put the first scheduled flight on hold, but not even weather and delays together

can wither the enthusiasm of the spectators. Their virtue is rewarded just before sunset as Tony the Tiger and Mickey Mouse ("Earforce One"), the cat and mouse Hares for the Hare and Hounds race, take shape before their very eyes, growing noses, sprouting ears. The heads of the cartoon animals lift upright to cheers and clapping, rise off the ground and drift, smiling, over thousands of wide eyes and animated faces. All up and down the airstrip, against a hazy Michigan sunset, the other balloons inflate, rise upright, and lift off downwind in pursuit of the cat and mouse.

For most pilots, the Battle Creek event, like the championship meet at Indianola, means competition, the skillful piloting of a balloon to perform a series of tasks with the greatest possible precision. One of the most serious and accomplished balloon competitors is Bruce Comstock, six-time winner of the National Championship and winner of the 1981 World Championship held at Battle Creek. His soft-spoken view of competition is belied by his own championship record. "In the early days of ballooning," he says, "there were some people who thought balloon competition was dangerous and wanted to ban it. I think you ought to do what you want to do. People who just enjoy flying balloons and enjoy the natural beauty involved in ballooning and have no urge to compete shouldn't compete. I think, though, that people who haven't flown competitively and don't know if they want to do it, ought to try it. There's something magical about it that you can't experience any other way. It's a lot of work, and there are so many things that go wrong on every flight, but it's a big thrill if you do it well."

Later in the week, after a variety of competitive tasks and a number of scrubbed flights, the cat and mouse are back for a Balloon Glow and fireworks, grinning through light, waving in the wind.

Snowmass Balloon Festival

Aspen, Colorado   •   July 8-10   •   50 Balloons   •   Begun 1971

Year after year, a small group of balloonists gathers high in the Colorado Rockies to enjoy a weekend of fun-flying in clear mountain air. Up in the Aspen valley, the air is cool, the ascents are easy, the burns are few, the fuel lasts, and the long flights are over terrain that enchants the eye and soothes the soul.

The first flight, beginning before dawn, is a distance task from the Aspen Airport down the valley toward Glenwood Springs, the flock of balloons gliding together over mountain meadows, wooded hills, between distant ranges of ragged, snow-capped peaks. Some pilots descend to skim the surface of ponds, touching down in the reflected colors of their own balloons. One pilot, some say, lands his balloon on the patio of a hillside house, and in a reversal of

tradition, accepts a glass of champagne from the owner. The others move on, mile after mile riding the currents of air. Beneath the balloons, a herd of elk crosses a clearing.

Popping toy balloons with nails on sticks is the task assigned the following morning. The party balloons are attached to poles at each corner of the launch area, and the challenge for a pilot is to find the winds which will carry his or her own hot air balloon from point to point around the field. The hot air balloons circle for hours on the "box" winds of the valley, one pilot scoring three hits.

In the afternoon, children are given tethered rides in a unicorn balloon, a mythical beast rising dreamlike in a far valley.

Ron McCain 199

Calgary Stampede Balloon Race

Calgary, Alberta   •   July 8-17   •   30 Balloons   •   Begun 1974

"Howdy folks. Welcome to Calgary. Roundup time." As States travelers emerge from Canadian customs and pass through the doors into a welcoming corral in the Calgary air terminal, a cowboy ropes them and a cowgirl brands them on the back of a hand with a red rubber stamp.

The "Greatest Outdoor Show on Earth" began whooping and hollering in 1912. In the early years of modern hot air ballooning, Dale Lang, one of Canada's few pilots at that time, persuaded the Stampede Board to allow balloons to fly out of the infield of the grounds. Each year, he was joined by more and more pilots until so many wanted to participate that the launch area was moved up to Scotchman's Hill, overlooking the Stampede Grounds. Every weather-permitting evening of the Stampede, the balloonists gather on the hill with the people who come there to get a free but distant look at the rodeo without shelling out an admission fee. The Alberta Free Balloon Society chose the site so that the balloons could fly over the grandstand during the famous Chuck Wagon races, but the winds of the Alberta prairie blow any direction they damned well please.

At the pilot briefing center, weather announcements often begin jokingly with a consultation of Weather Rock, a rock suspended by a string from a pole attached to a wooden base. On the base is a typed sign reading:

> If rock is wet, it's raining.
> If rock is not wet, it's not raining.
> If rock is swinging, it's windy.
> If rock is not swinging, it may be calm.
> If there is a shadow, it is sunny.

If the Calgary rock were outside, it would often be swinging. Several briefings end with the Balloonmeister, wearing a cowboy hat, saying, "Well, it looks like the rock wins tonight. Next briefing is 6:30 tomorrow afternoon."

Calgary pilots believe they are "more aggressive" than balloonists from other areas because of the conditions they fly in, launching in stronger winds and taking the consequences when landing. Balloonists from other areas point out that Calgary pilots have millions of flat Alberta acres to land on, unlike, say, balloonists from the Northeastern U.S., who learn to look for clearings in wooded hills. The Calgary balloonists do have a wild and windy feel about them. One of them tells of getting caught in a cold front while flying. While "screaming over the ground," he said, he remembered a cartoon of a cowboy dropping over a cliff on his horse, straining against the reins and yelling, "Whoaza, you sonofagun, whoaza!" His laughter did not necessarily reassure his passenger. Nor did his long drag through thistles. But the adventure left them both none the worse for wear and with a rousing story to tell their friends.

Only a fraction of scheduled launches were made during the Calgary Winter Olympics earlier in the year, and now, during Stampede week, more are winded out. One evening, the balloon crews entertain themselves with a scavenger hunt, searching for such items as "organic Frisbees" and "July snowballs." Another night, many pilots and crew members spend their free time taking in the Chuck Wagon races down at the grandstand.

Throughout the days, the Stampede roars on. Bronco busting, steer roping, bulldogging, square dancing outside City Hall and in Rope Square. Kids Day is highlighted with ostrich chariot races, youngsters riding sheep, and a performance by "Canada's first and only machete juggler."

On an afternoon favorable for ballooning, a wagon train of balloon vehicles rolls up to Scotchman's Hill and circles on the crest. During inflation, the breeze freshens, and lift-offs are brisk. One balloon shoots off over the roof of the park pavilion, the launch field dropping away and sliding off to the west, the Stampede grandstand and grounds receding towards the ragged horizon of the Canadian Rockies. As the balloons move over the sprawling city, a pilot points to the needle of Calgary Tower, says he passed by it so closely during the Winter Olympics that he could see people eating in the skytop restaurant. They were surprised to see him, he says. Some waved.

The balloon passes over the Bow River, the island of the Calgary Zoo, Deerfoot Trail freeway, over suburban neighborhoods and out to the green and yellow patchwork prairie. Off to the right, a green balloon skims along above the rolling ground, the two balloons following the contours of the earth. Miles from the city, after an hour and a half in the air, the pilot chooses a country road for a landing spot. "Face forward, bend your knees," he says, a field streaming away beneath the basket. And then the sudden jolting stop on the lip of the roadway. Mosquitoes are waiting for the visitors. After the chase crew arrives and the balloon is packed into the vehicle, the pilot brings out a small table covered with a checkered tablecloth and sets it with brass goblets. The pilot pours champagne to celebrate the flight. Then there's a cold return ride to the city through the dark in the back of a pickup.

200

Canadian Fantasy Festival

Barrie, Ontario • July 15-21 • 40 Balloons • Begun 1984

"The best pilots are always on the ground," says a veteran pilot, referring to the advantage spectators have over pilots at a competitive balloon event.

At Molson Park, outside Barrie, Ontario, forty miles north of Toronto, the spectators watch the competition balloons fly to the field. From their vantage point on the ground, the spectators watch the balloons approach, and when a balloon floats toward the target – the pilot leaning out over the gondola, swinging the baggie, deciding which moment is the best to release the marker – the crowd gladly helps, shouting, "Now! Drop it now!" More often than not, the pilot continues swinging the marker a few more seconds before releasing it, seeming to the crowd to have waited too long. "It looks different from up there," one of the pilots says.

With pilots participating in multiple judge-declared goals, a fishing derby, a key grab, and other tasks, the spectators have many opportunities to be lawn-chair pilots – and to appreciate the skill of competitive flying. What they see, though, is only a small part of the total task. Before one event, pilots across the field study the ascent of helium balloons and consult navigational maps spread out on the ground or on the hoods of chase vehicles. Meanwhile, a Swedish pilot lies on his back in the grass, hands behind his head, seeming to be in reverie, but actually watching the directions of wind-driven clouds at different altitudes, a habit of his Viking ancestors. After plotting their ideal launch sites, the crews drive from the field and into the countryside, stopping from time to time to inflate and release helium balloons and chart their course, all the while alert to wind shifts and to the time restrictions of the launch window. After a final launch spot is selected, a crew member acquires permission from the landowner, and pre-flight preparations begin. By the time the spectators back at the field see the balloons rising in the distance, the major strategic choices have already been made.

During the " box task," the crowd first sees a single balloon approach the field at a high altitude, followed by other competitors. In the distance, the first balloon vents heavily, dropping to a lower altitude and to a wind current which carries it back to the field, close to the "X." As the pilot swings the marker, the crowd coaxes him when to throw. A toss near the "X" draws applause. Another balloon drifts away from the field, out of range, and the spectators watch the sky for balloon after balloon to approach. During one fly-in event, they see a masterful venting from a high altitude, the envelope distorting, and a glide right over the "X."

For the fishing derby, a single passenger in each basket is trussed into a harness and provided with a net on a long aluminum handle. Among thousands of helium-filled toy balloons inflated in a tent are several mylar "fish." The balloonists are to launch off-site, calculating to fly above the balloon tent at the precise moment the helium balloons are released. Anyone netting a fish will receive $25,000. The ideal launch spot, though, turns out to be directly in line with a radio tower, just outside the minimum distance from the field. Most of the pilots pass over the helium-balloon tent several minutes before the scheduled release. Only one balloon – which launches from beside the base of the tower – flies directly over the tent at the moment the helium balloons spread into the sky. Even then, the chances of netting a helium fish are astronomical, and all the balloons float up and away. Later, during the key-grab event, the wind shifts direction after the balloons are in the air, and no one flies even close.

Not all is competition at the meet. Between burns at the Balloon Glow one evening, a pilot tells of landing on the grounds of a nursing home after the morning flight that day and taking residents up for tethered rides. When one elderly lady was disembarking from the basket after a second ride, the pilot asked her if she would like to go up a third time. "Not unless you untie those ropes holding us down," she said.

Watching fireworks after the Balloon Glow, one woman spectator turns to another and says, "This fantasy festival really is well named, isn't it?"

On the Air

At daybreak on a still, misty morning, crews walk eighteen red, white, and blue balloons from one end of a Michigan field to the other, moving quietly through beams of sunlight filtered through trees beside the site. The crews group the balloons together, and the envelopes stand motionless, watched by only a handful of people standing outside the field. Off at one edge of the site, a helicopter with a yard-wide sphere attached to its side lifts off the ground like an insect and whirrs away over trees, returns, circles the balloons again and again. One balloon rises, the other balloons silently following it as though attached with threads. The balloons ascend in a cluster until a current of wind spreads them, carries them like floating corks. The helicopter circles the balloons in ever-widening rings, then weaves its way among them as they drift away.

Held midway through the standard balloon meet season, this is a balloon event with a difference. Although there are no spectators, millions of people across the United States and Canada will later see the filmed flight on television commercials. The image of the red, white, and blue RE/MAX balloon is a corporate logo, and RE/MAX balloons themselves are fitting subjects for use in advertising. Oldsmobile, Chevron, Stroh's, Budweiser, Pepsi, Coca Cola, 7-Up, Shell, Kellogg's, Post, and scores of other businesses large and small choose balloons as an advertising medium, a particularly pleasing form of advertising which reaches thousands of people for a relatively low cost. Since the first RE/MAX balloon appeared at the Albuquerque Balloon Fiesta in 1978, the fleet, comprised of scores of balloons, has become what is believed to be the largest corporate balloon fleet anywhere.

The filming of eighteen balloons lifting off and in flight presented several challenges to filmmaker Don Spencer. "First, we're totally at the mercy of the weather, of wind conditions," Spencer says the day before the first scheduled flight. "Obviously, we want skies with white puffs of cloud, but as anybody familiar with ballooning knows, we'll get what we get." During an unusually hot and dry summer, preliminary crews reported a week ahead of the shoot that Michigan fields were brown with drought.

"Weather is only the first problem," Spencer says. "This may be the most difficult film footage ever attempted with balloons. Not only do you have to coordinate eighteen balloons in their rise, get them to stack nice, get their logos towards camera, all with the wind working in your favor, but you need to get them to hold together long enough before they begin to spread out."

Achieving that choreography, Spencer points out, will require the dovetailing of skills of sets of people not accustomed to working together. "There are three distinct groups," Spencer says, "which need to be coordinated: the pilots, the two camera crews on the ground, and the helicopter pilot and cameraman. All need to understand each other enough to cooperate to achieve the magic thirty-second moment we want to capture on film."

To acquire that footage, Spencer has rented a rare gyroscopic camera noted for its ability to rotate full-circle and to zoom in from a vast background down to the smallest detail. "One of the sequences it has done," Spencer says, "is to move from a panoramic shot of a mountain range down to a single cabin in those mountains, to a window in the cabin, to a stove inside, and to a teapot steaming on the stove."

Ed Dosien

The camera arrived only days before the scheduled shoot. Spencer hired a noted cameraman to operate the helicopter camera and a pilot experienced with such cameras to fly the helicopter. The cameraman and the pilot have never worked together before. The night before the first scheduled flight, Spencer meets with the cameraman and explains to him what set of images he wants on film.

A downpour that night causes concern that the launch field might be too muddy, but the rain is also welcomed as a relief from heat and perhaps as a greening agent. The morning is clear and still. The ground camera crews are the first to arrive at the launch area, on the grounds of a balloon manufacturing company. As they stand out in the wet weeds before dawn, one of the crew says to another: "It's like hunting, this getting up early and standing in the dark."

At the pilot briefing in a tent set up beside the field, the site director announces that the condition of the launch area is acceptable in spite of the rain, and that the weather is favorable for flying. Spencer tells the pilots: "I am looking for thirty seconds of film capturing the first moments of separation after a slow balloon ascent. That's the shot, the magic moment. The rest is gravy." An ascent of fifty feet per minute up to an altitude of 500 feet will allow the helicopter cameraman to get that shot, Spencer says. The pilots are given different colored streamers for color-coding the balloons to allow the filmmaker to contact any particular balloon by radio and to prevent a chase crew nightmare.

Pilots and crews proceed to the launch field and, at sunup, on signal, begin inflation. The helicopter is late. By the time it arrives, the balloons have been standing upright for nearly half an hour, using valuable propane. The sky is clouding over. After the helicopter arrives and is prepared to begin shooting, the balloons are given the signal to lift off. They do, first some, then others, more, the group of balloons spreading out immediately.

That night, during another rain, Spencer sees the black-and-white takes, is disappointed. Realizing more communication is needed between film crew and balloon pilots, he appoints a single pilot to ascend first, establishing the rate of ascent, controlling the clustered rise of the others.

The evening rain greens the landscape even more, and the moisture in the air creates early morning fog. Dawn breaks on a misty morning and pristine sky, ideal shooting conditions. The pilots have been instructed to stay together by following the leader balloon, and the helicopter pilot and the cameraman have now had an hour of working together. Lighting considerations prompt Spencer to instruct the balloon crews to move the balloons to the other end of the field. All is at last ready for camera and action. Radio commands are given to the pilot of the leader balloon. Following him, the other balloons rise slowly as a single entity, separate at a single altitude, float over wooded hills and lakes covered with a light ground fog shining with sunlight.

At the pilot banquet that evening, Spencer thanks the balloonists for their crucial work in what he calls the "Miracle Morning." The following night, a tornado sweeps through the area with a thundering green sky flashing with lightning, and the next morning is rain.

U.S. National Hot Air Balloon Championship

Indianola, Iowa　　•　　July 29-August 6　　•　　135 Balloons　　•　　Begun 1970

Faces scrubbed and glowing with Iowa heat fill the midway past concessions of Iowa Butterflied Pork Chops, Iowa Beef, Fresh Iowa Sweet Corn. At one end of the midway is grassy shade under black walnut trees, their leaves singing with locusts. Some spectators have claimed the premium shade with lawn chairs and blankets, while others sit right out in the sun on a hillside sloping down from the midway, overlooking the natural amphitheater of the fenced-off launch and target area on the next hill. At the edges of the hot, pale sky, hazy mountains of clouds spread across the horizon. It is the opening afternoon of the national championships, a ballooning event as traditional to Indianola as the Iowa feast of sweet corn and catfish.

First held in Des Moines in 1970, the U.S. Nationals moved the next year to the farm town of Indianola, where it has remained up to 1988, famous among pilots for thousands of eager volunteers, Iowa hospitality, and non-air-conditioned dormitory rooms at Simpson College. After years of debate, the sponsoring Balloon Federation of America has chosen to shift the annual competition to Baton Rouge, Louisiana, for a period of three years. More sophisticated lodging and more prize money are greeted with enthusiasm by many pilots, while others regret leaving a site rich with friendships and memories. Some think the move is only temporary, that the Nationals may one day return to Indianola. In the meantime, the town retains its ballooning tradition, highlighting the week's events with the opening of the permanent facility of the National Balloon Museum and announcing that the Nationals will be replaced by a new ten-day event, the National Balloon Classic.

Balloon politics are irrelevant to the spectators on opening day as bright fiesta balloons bloom out of the prairie grass and one by one rise up and over the crowd and the walnut trees at the top of the hill. Gaping, snapshots, and applause accompany the announcer's introduction of each balloon and balloon pilot passing overhead, balloons with names like airborne racehorses: "Luck of the Irish," "Odyssey," "Just a Dream," "Song Breeze," "Raspberry Sunrise," "Lunar Magic," "Thunder Bucket," "Quo Vadis," "Misty Morn." The first of the competition balloons approaches through the humid sunset of a blistering day. The pilot deftly maneuvers down through levels of soft wind, and drops a marker on the "X," drawing applause from the crowd. The hazy sun seems to draw the remaining movement of the air down with it, leaving distant balloons suspended in a static sky. The crowd remains, waiting through dusk for a few returning balloons to inflate again for a Balloon Glow.

Politics seem far away, too, days later, after more heat and few flights, when pilots and crews mix with area farmers, Simpson professors, and local businesspeople at Farmer's Appreciation Night at the Pilot's Compound. Members of the Warren County Cattlemen's Association flip hamburgers from smoking grills. Inside the briefing center, which is throbbing with the music of a Country Western band, farmers and pilots line the long tables, enjoying heaping plates of hamburgers, cole slaw, tomatoes, and plastic cups of foaming beer. A red-cheeked, white-haired farmer in a fresh, long-sleeved dress shirt sits, smoking a cigar, looking across the room to the band playing "Blue Suede Shoes." Beside him, his wife is tapping her knee in rhythm.

Atlanta Balloon Festival

Lawrenceville, Georgia   •   August 5-7   •   60 Balloons   •   One-time event

Each afternoon, the clouds build in the heat, and the turbulence cracks into thunderstorms. The mornings, though, are clear, attracting thousands of Atlanta-area spectators to the Gwinnett County Airport for the balloon launches and airshows of the TV5 Great Balloon Festival.

On one of the mornings, fresh from rain the night before, the pattern is familiar to balloon festival-goers: Spectators gather around a launch area in pre-dawn darkness. Pilots and crews from a pilot briefing drive onto the airstrip. A voice comes over the PA, welcoming the crowd and explaining the process they are about to see. The blast of a burner and a stream of fire in the thinning dark draw gasps from the crowd. Crews walk out envelopes onto the concrete, the fabric colors pale in the faint light. The excitement of the crowd grows with the start-up of inflator fans, grows in intensity right along with sunrise and with the expanding envelopes, which are billowing with color across the launch area. The sound of the crowd increases as the envelopes stand upright and crescendos with the balloons rising into the air. The balloons float away, the chase vehicles drive off in pursuit, and the crowd leaves the airstrip. What was empty and quiet before daybreak, then filled with sound and moving color at dawn, is now, in the morning sunlight, empty and quiet once more, as though nothing has occurred there at all.

The midway is packed throughout the day, and the highlight of the early afternoons is the heart-stopping aerobatics of airshow pilots looping and rolling their planes across the sky. Clouds build, the heat rises, the red Georgia clay beyond the launch site shines in the stormy light, and the kudzu vines droop heavily over the trees at the edge of the airfield parking lot.

The next morning, the sun glows through light mist, and the balloons fly again, to the loud delight of the spectators.

Ed Dosien

Festival de Montgolfières

Saint-Jean-sur-Richelieu, Quebec • August 13-21 • 145 Balloons • Begun 1984

Ed Dosien

It's half an hour's drive from Montreal, across the St. Lawrence River and through farm country, to St-Jean-sur-Richelieu, the Capitale des Montgolfieres. St-Jean community groups established the Festival du Montgolfieres to bring economic growth to the region, and the mayor of St-Jean, Delbert Deschambault, enthusiastically concurs that their North American Championship meet has done just that. "The meet has put us on the map," Deschambault says, explaining what a balloon festival can do for a community.

"It used to be that people from the States would pass right through here on their way to Montreal," he says. "Now, they stop, about 300,000 people in nine days, bringing half a million dollars directly into our economy. Investors have also become interested in us, establishing new businesses here and making us one of the fastest developing cities of our size in the province of Quebec. With the 1991 World Balloon Championships scheduled to be held here, plans are underway for expansion of accommodations. The smaller hotels in the area are already booked solid during every festival. All this growth is making people proud of their city and their region, so that more and more people are volunteering their time and services to the festival and other community activities. Our people are speaking more English, the better to greet our tourist friends, and many entrepreneurial businesses have sprung up here, from horse and buggy rides to the making and selling of miniature hot air balloons. The meets have activated all kinds of businesses, and not only for a nine-day period once a year, but year-round. We now have balloons through our skies even in winter. Overall, what our festival has done is shift the task of community development onto the citizens. That makes the job of mayor so much easier."

Although the first morning of the festival is weathered out, and the afternoon is threatening, the crowds arrive. Looking up at a cluster of attached kites swooping and soaring against the gray sky, a Quebec pilot says, "Good weather for kites is bad weather for balloons." A few balloons inflate and tether for the crowd. After packing up, the pilot with an eye for kites brings out his own rectangular kite, controlled by strings attached to each corner, and wrestles it around the sky.

In the Tente de Briefing the next day, pilots and crew step around puddles from heavy rain to get to picnic tables and chairs for bilingual briefings, but as the days pass, morale rises with better weather and scheduled flights.

A crowd gets what it comes for one cool, breezy morning, when the balloons, as though choreographed, inflate and launch to "Bolero," "Tales from the Vienna Woods," "The Planets," "Star Wars." As is usual, the special shapes inflate last, the dinosaur's head growing from the ground, one eye cracking open as the monster swells, the mouth gaping wide, showing its great white teeth. The pink and white elephant lumbers itself up off the ground, its trunk and legs waving in the wind. "Dino" rises to a virtuoso trumpet solo of "Funiculi Funicula."

In the Tente de Biere that evening, one of the pilots who has guided the green monster through the air tells of landing it in a twenty-knot wind, one of its legs folding under the basket. With the cloth between the basket and a smooth, grassy field, the basket "slid along as if on glass." Seeing only fabric and not knowing what he might slide into at any moment, the pilot frantically tried to pull the leg free. The beast at last came to rest at one end of the field, short of a fence, holding the wicker gondola in one paw, its toenails curled around the rim.

From the dark midway, the lighted tents of white and red stripes, white and yellow, white and blue, white and green, glow like paper lanterns.

Albuquerque Balloon Fiesta

Albuquerque, New Mexico　•　October 1-9　•　600 Balloons　•　Begun 1972

From a multi-colored balloon-shaped *pinata* hanging from a chandelier in a motel lobby at the north end of town to a balloon-shaped bunch of red chiles hanging in the doorway of a shop down in Old Town, Albuquerque lets its visitors know it is the Balloon Capital of the World, hosting the largest gathering of hot air balloons ever held anywhere.

What essentially began with a single balloon at an aircraft party hosted by aviator Sid Cutter in 1971 has become a gigantic festival highlighted by weekend mass ascensions of nearly six hundred balloons, attended by about a million spectators over the nine-day event. "The Big One," the climatic festival of the ballooning season, truly lives up to its name.

The freeway drivers creeping along bumper to bumper through the six o'clock darkness the first morning of the fiesta know the event is big. They look past the jammed lanes of the freeway to a searchlight beam waving through the dark, then see fireworks blossoming and showering over the distant launch field. In the fiesta parking lot half an hour later, they hear the horns and drums of a high school band opening the festivities. The latecomers wedge through the midway crowd. Over heads, concession signs invite spectators to enjoy Breakfast Burritos, Green Chile Stew. The mass of people spreads across the acres of launch area, parting around laid-out envelopes streaming with color across the sandy ground. The light above Sandia Peak glows with coming sunrise.

Trailing a ribbon of pink smoke, the leader balloon lifts off. Envelopes ripple, heave, roll with air to the roaring of inflators, hundreds of balloons in the first wave growing, unfurling, rising with the blasts of burners, the downwind balloons lifting, seeming to pull the next ones up behind them, a stream of color flowing up and curving with the wind. As each balloon lifts off farther down the field, another envelope is unrolled in the place it left. By the time the last balloons lift from the far end of the field, the balloons downwind are standing, and when the last of the first wave passes overhead, the second wave rises back down the length of the field, followed by the third

wave, until balloons fill the sky from the field itself to the southern horizon.

The chase vehicles which retrieve the balloons in the morning creep down Central Avenue as parade floats in the afternoon, crews cavorting through downtown Albuquerque in the Balloon Fiesta Parade as the costumed Blue-Loon Loonies, Balloon on the Moon. One memorable balloonist masquerades as a saguaro cactus. During the Oktoberfest award ceremonies at Civic Plaza, the end of the parade route, a German oom-pah-pah band, in lederhosen, reveals its true identity by breaking out into *mariachi* music.

The morning of the second mass ascension, under stars and a bright moon, an early crowd rises to consciousness on the midway, drinking coffee and eating cinnamon rolls, breakfast burritos. Beyond the rich smells of food concession stands, one catches whiffs of propane from the adjacent launch area. A green and white Dawn Patrol balloon of chevron design glows in muted burner flashes above the silhouetted Sandia Mountains. Again, a mass ascension of a magnitude never seen before this fiesta: waves and waves of color. This time, though, the balloons are able to use the famed "Albuquerque Box," launching, drifting south toward the city, rising into a northern current of wind at a higher altitude, and returning high across the field, even as the later waves of balloons rise from the desert, a continuous, circular flow of aerostats.

By five o'clock that afternoon, chase vehicles pull onto the field for a Balloon Glow briefing, a detailed explanation of the nine burns comprising the one-hour spectacle of glowing envelopes. Three of the radio commands will be for all-burns, and the other six will be for designated balloons burning in each individual glow, creating patterns of light. After sunset, tens of thousands of spectators are wandering among shadowy, standing envelopes, a forest of balloons in a desert, fireflies of pilot lights blinking through the dusk. In darkness, the crowd joins in a countdown, burners blast, and the forest lights.

Above, an airplane pilot looks down upon a garden of glowing balloons surrounded by dots of light spreading to the edges of the desert city.

Ed Dosien

Glossary

Aerostat – A lighter-than-air device: hot air balloons, gas balloons, and dirigibles. **Aerostation** is the science and art of operating such a vehicle, and an **aeronaut** is the "air-sailor" who pilots a lighter-than-air craft.

Baggie – A bean-bag marker, with cloth streamer, for scoring in competitive events. Tossed, in flight, toward a cloth "X" **target** on the ground.

Balloon Crew – A group of about four people who function both as **ground crew**, helping with pre-flight preparations, and **chase crew**, retrieving the balloon after its flight and packing it back onto the chase vehicle.

Balloon Glow – Also known as **Nightglow**, the crowd-pleasing random or synchronized blast of burners to illuminate a group of balloons after dark. Begun near Albuquerque as a Christmas Eve festivity.

Balloon Basket – Also, **gondola**. Most commonly made of wicker or aluminum, it carries the pilot, passengers, and a variety of equipment, including: an **altimeter**, a **variometer** (rate-of-climb meter), a **pyrometer** (gauge registering temperature inside the crown of the balloon), a compass, fuel tanks, tool kit (with propane lighter). A wicker balloon basket is the most traditional part of the modern hot air balloon.

Balloonmeister – The person responsible for every phase of flight operations at a balloon meet. Approves or cancels any given flight, depending upon weather conditions. Directs an operations staff of **Weather Officer, Safety Officer, Launch Director**, and **Launch Officials.**

Box – Flying back and forth over the same area by using winds of opposite directions at different altitudes. A common phenomenon in valleys because of drainage of air down mountains. The "Albuquerque Box" is the best-known.

Burners – The fuel-burning source of power which is essential to the modern hot air balloon, consisting of coil tubing and a fuel-ejecting nozzle. A double burner system generates 24 million BTUs per hour. A pilot **burns** by turning or pulling the **blast valve.**

Chase Vehicle – The truck, van, or trailer carrying the balloon components, pilot, and crew. Frequently painted with corporate, commercial, or personal designs.

Christening – A traditional ballooning ceremony in which **first riders** are baptized with champagne while the pilot recites the "Balloonist's Prayer."

Competitive Tasks – A variety of events which test pilot skill. The **Hare and Hounds, Judge-Declared Goals**, and **Pilot-Declared Goals** are performed away from the launch site, while **CNTEs (Controlled Navigational Trajectory Events)** are **fly-in tasks**, which bring the balloons back over the launch area in clear view of spectators. A particularly popular event is the **Key Grab**, in which pilots try to snatch a set of car keys from atop a pole, thus winning a car.

Corporate Balloons – Balloons used as a form of advertising.

Crown – The top center point of a balloon envelope, also known as the **apex**. Attached to the crown is the **crownline**, which a crew member holds taut when the balloon is being inflated, preventing oscillation of the envelope.

Deflation – A hot-air balloon pilot deflates the envelope by **ripping out** the top panel, the **deflation port**, of the balloon with a **ripcord**, or **deflation line**.

Distortion – The variation of the standard inflated shape of a balloon, caused during inflation by strong winds, or during flight by the **venting** of hot air from the envelope, or by **wind sheers. Spinnakering** is a sailing term for the distortion of an envelope being inflated or tethered in a high wind.

Envelope – The fabric bubble of modern rip-stop nylon or other synthetic material. **Load tapes** running vertically down the envelope end in cables which attach to the basket's uprights.

Festival – One of many names for a hot-air balloon **meet** or **rally**. Other names include **Balloonfest, Classic, Fiesta, Race**, or **Stampede**. A hot-air balloon **Championship** tends to be a more formally competitive and controlled event.

Fiesta Flying – **Fun-flying**, not structured by competition. **Fiesta balloons** are balloons not participating in competition.

Free Flight – Untethered. A balloon drifting with the wind.

Inflation – The filling of an envelope with cold air from an **inflator fan** and hot air from burners. After the envelope is about seventy-five percent filled with cold air, hot inflation begins.

Laying Out – A ground crew's **walking** a balloon envelope out of its bag and spreading out the fabric, readying it for inflation. Part of the pre-flight assembly of a balloon.

Maneuvering Vent – A slit in the side of the balloon envelope, opened by the **venting line** for the spilling of hot air from the envelope. **Venting** enables the balloon to descend faster than it would by the cooling of the air inside the envelope. Corporate pilots often vent in order to rotate the balloon, turning a company logo on the envelope toward a crowd.

Montgolfiere – The generic word for the hot air balloon, named for its inventors, Joseph and Etienne Montgolfier. **Charliere** is the rarely used term for the gas balloon, named after its inventor, Jacques Alexandre Cesar Charles. The first two manned flights in history were in the two kinds of balloons. The hot air balloon flew first, November 20, 1783, and the gas balloon flew ten days later.

Pibal – A helium-filled **pilot balloon** released to ascertain the directions and velocities of wind at different altitudes.

Pilot Packs – The package of local information, maps, activity tickets, and giveaways pilots receive when registering for a meet.

PZs – **Prohibited Zones**. Also known as **Restricted Areas** and **Red Zones**, areas in which balloonists are not to land.

Special Shapes – Balloons of other than standard shape. Particularly popular among balloon-meet crowds. Said to be the direction of the future for hot air balloons, especially corporate balloons.

Splash and Dash – A maneuver in which a pilot tests his or her flying skill by descending to the surface of a body of water, touches the water with the basket, and ascends again. Other exercises are **tree-topping**, touching the tops of trees in flight, and **kissing**, touching the envelope of another balloon in flight.

Sport Balloons – Multi-colored, non-corporate balloons, designed for fun-flying or competition.

Tether – A secured line restricting the ascent of a balloon. Frequently used by corporate pilots to give short rides to the public.

Thermals – Updrafts caused by heated air rising from the ground. By flying early in the morning or late in the afternoon, balloonists avoid these potentially dangerous conditions.

Throat – The **mouth** of a balloon envelope, usually bordered by a **skirt** or **scoop** to help direct the heat of the burners into the envelope.

Winds Aloft – The winds at different altitudes.

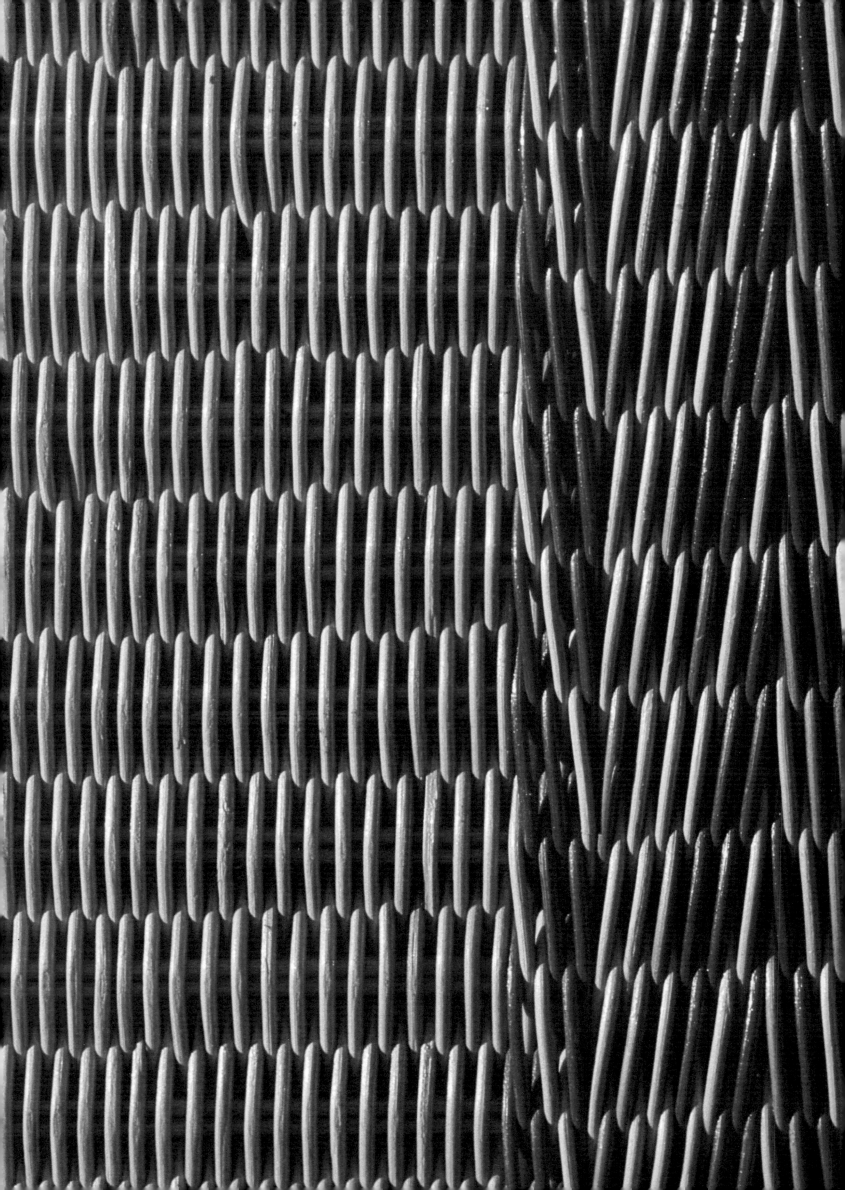